How'd I Get Here?

And Why Am I Stealing M&M's From Air Force One?

Dan Beckmann

NEW YORK

How'd I Get Here?
And Why Am I Stealing M&M's From Air Force One?

Published in New York, New York, by Morgan James Publishing. Morgan James and The Entrepreneurial Publisher are trademarks of Morgan James, LLC. www.MorganJamesPublishing.com

The Morgan James Speakers Group can bring authors to your live event. For more information or to book an event visit The Morgan James Speakers Group at www.TheMorganJamesSpeakersGroup.com.

BitLit
FOR ALL THE BOOKS YOU OWN

FREE eBook edition for your
existing eReader with purchase

PRINT NAME ABOVE

For more information,
instructions, restrictions, and
to register your copy, go to
www.bitlit.ca/readers/register
or use your QR Reader to scan
the barcode:

ISBN 978-1-63047-056-2 paperback
ISBN 978-1-63047-057-9 eBook
ISBN 978-1-63047-058-6 hardcover
Library of Congress Control Number:
2013957034

Cover Design by:
Chris Treccani
www.3dogdesign.net

Interior Design by:
Bonnie Bushman
bonnie@caboodlegraphics.com

In an effort to support local communities, raise awareness and funds, Morgan James Publishing donates a percentage of all book sales for the life of each book to Habitat for Humanity Peninsula and Greater Williamsburg.

Get involved today, visit
www.MorganJamesBuilds.com

Habitat
for Humanity
Peninsula and
Greater Williamsburg
Building Partner

For those who raised me:

Grampa…always my best man. Gran…who taught me the meaning of "a really good piece of coffee." And my mom…for her years of collecting yardsticks and wooden spoons, while always showing great restraint for not using them on me…or at least not very often. LOL

Table of Contents

Acknowledgments

(You actually *may* want to read this part …)

Not long ago, I received an email from a friend titled, "*Rosary Card.*" I wasn't positive rosaries came in the form of cards. I was, however, absolutely certain that news of such a thing wasn't email-worthy. Even so, I clicked "open."

"*Hey, I can't remember ever having a Rosary Card,*" I wrote, "*but growing up Catholic, I can tell you how important my Rosary was to me. I clung to it, prayed on it, and wore it around my neck. Once, while in detention in Catholic school, I made a candy necklace out of one. Wrapping bubble gum around each bead...going so far as to have the 4th Hail Mary slightly lodged in my throat. It was an uncomfortable feeling, and a bit embarrassing, to say the least. Half a dozen detentions and three bruised knuckles later, the nuns are still talking about it! Please take plenty of pictures of your Rosary Card for me. I hope you find the color you want. And please, for the love of all that's holy, don't put it in your mouth. Trust me.*"

Later that evening my friend emailed again, this time, to tell me she hadn't heard of Rosary Cards either. She wasn't even Catholic. Although, her meeting at the *Rotary Club* did, in fact, go very well.

So that's me. The "me" who has the attention span of a gnat—the "me" who took four years to write this book—and the "me" who spent forty-plus years experiencing its content.

There have been numerous people along the way who helped make all these stories possible. I certainly didn't want to leave anyone out. So, instead of running the risk of forgetting about that second cousin, twice removed, who lives in Des Moines, whom I've never met but will surely be upset because I accidentally omitted his/her name, I decided to include all the names ever created, according to "The Google."

It was also a shameless effort to add more pages to this book, thus giving the impression I did more work than I actually had.

I intended to list the names in alphabetical order. And, in another attempt to go one step further, designed a clever scheme to increase the font size. Adding even more pages.

However, by the time I reached the letter "G," it was clear I had more pages than The Bible and *War and Peace* combined. I would fool no one. Therefore, I felt it best to cover everyone in the simplest of ways:

I wish to thank everybody from A'ishah to Zyana.

Chances are your name falls in between there somewhere. If not, blame the Internet. I've done the best I can.

DB

Falsehoods and Liberties

Fact and Fiction

(Stuff I had to tell you to make my lawyer, accountant, and priest feel better.)

1. I don't really have a priest.
2. According to the Guinness Book of World records, the world's tallest man in recorded history was Robert Wadlow of Alton, Illinois. On June 27, 1940, eight days before his death, Robert was measured at a staggering 8 feet, 11.1 inches. Despite having been known as the "Alton Giant," Robert was a kind and gentle man. This is most definitely different from Zeke, the troubled provocateur who lived in the trailer park below my street, and whom I falsely describe in Chapter 1 as being near 8 foot tall. He wasn't. But he seemed like that to me.
3. Two relatives did, in fact, die at my mom's table. There was a good bit of debate as to whether or not I should call it the "Death Table" or the more ominous, "Table of Death." The

latter seemed too sinister. Not to mention, the phrase "Table of Death" implies that more than two persons have perished at its edge. At the time of this book's publication, *only* two have died while sitting at it. So, until more shuffle off this mortal coil while sitting there, it shall remain, simply, the Death Table.

4. In the chapter titled *Music Mayhem*, I wrongfully imply that the interview set I created for Rod Stewart "would have made *The Today Show* proud." In all actuality, they would have been terribly disappointed had they seen my creation. I did not carry makeup. There was no hairspray for Mr. Stewart, and nowhere in sight was there a person waving feverishly at my camera from behind a glass window while holding a homemade sign that read, "Hi, Mom! I'm in NYC!"

5. In the chapter titled, *Spies, Lies, and Videotape*, I indicate that it is possible to make a fire while rubbing your hands together quickly. Although, I have seen it done many times in cartoons, I've never once been able to accomplish the feat myself. Having spent time in Cub Scouts as a kid, I couldn't do it with sticks either. Although, once, I did manage to see a spark while clicking two rocks together. That was just before I threw them at my friend Steve. I can't remember why. But that's beside the point.

6. I really did think Boy George was a girl. And that Jethro Tull was a character on The Beverly Hillbillies.

7. To the best of my knowledge, I am the only person I know of who has relieved himself at a urinal next to Tom Cruise *and* Walter Cronkite. Not at the same time, of course. That would be an entire book unto itself.

8. In 2003, the U.S. Supreme Court struck down sodomy laws nationwide. And, while some in South Carolina still believe they are not, in fact, a part of the Union, the ruling still applied

to them. You'll understand the relevance in the chapter titled, *Radio Dazed.*

9. I changed some names in a few strategic places throughout the book. No sense in embarrassing the producers who hired me … ruining their reputations with their respective clients. Especially since I was solely responsible for mangling their gigs. Also, a couple friends of mine have made some "minor" tax return errors. No need to point them out, either. They've been running for years, so why make it easier to locate them?

10. This literary narrative shouldn't be taken as totally literal. I've taken true pieces and parts and assembled them into savory stories. It's like a recipe, where I've arranged the ingredients into bite-sized tasty tales. It has all the good stuff … the same vitamins and minerals. You just won't feel so bloated from me serving up every detail.

A Note From
The Author

"…but ya gotta have faith, faith, faith!"
—George Michael

"Thelma and Louise-ing" myself off a cliff has always been easy for me. I jump—all the time—without ever knowing the trajectories, landing points, or even the height from which I'm about to free-fall. I never think about the crash below the cliff—just the feeling of freedom in flight between liftoff and the point where my bones break. I like to *do* … not *think and do*. Even with board games: playing chess requires too much thought … but checkers? Now, there ya go.

My wife Susan has always told me I have great faith. I didn't know anything about that. To my way of thinking, what she has always seen as faith was really a dash of impulsive behavior sprinkled with a tinge of over confidence.

A few years ago she told me about a test. "It's called a Spiritual Gifts test," she said. Her eyes lit up in that way that told me she had stumbled onto something she desperately wanted me to be a part of.

"Oh." I replied, disinterested, as I continued washing the dishes.

I'm kidding, of course. I've never washed a dish in my life. And I'd never heard of such a silly test.

Sensing my lack of enthusiasm she said, "Don't worry. There aren't any wrong answers."

The following morning, though it was Wednesday, Sue drove me to a local church. "It's just there, …" She pointed. "In that little building."

"What's *just there*?" I asked.

"Your Spiritual Gifts test," she said, her voice ringing that "don't-you-remember-we-talked-about-this" tone. "You take it right inside that office."

A flash of nervous energy (even more than my usual dosage) washed over me. This felt like my first day at Ortona Elementary all over again. The Post Traumatic School Disorder slowly resurfaced. "You were *serious* about that?"

"Here," she said, producing a pencil from her purse. "You'll need this."

I got out of the car and lumbered my way into the building. Once inside the "classroom," I wedged myself into a squeaky little school desk, then scooted me—and my wooden tutu—into a nice, safe place in the corner. Out of sight from the "teacher" sitting in judgment behind her oversized, mahogany desk. And away from the other "students" whose wives had tricked them into coming, as well.

I pulled the pencil from my pocket and decided it could use some sharpening. Managing to remove myself from the seat, I made my way to the front of the classroom. After inserting the pencil into the sharpener, I cranked the handle, noticed the #2 on the end as the shavings fell to the floor. And for a second, I found that "quietness" Yogis talk about – that "Zen Moment" spiritual leaders speak of.

It's amazing what pops into the mind during absolute quietness.

Whatever happened to #1 pencils, I thought as I walked back to my desk. Why had I never heard of them? Was the #1 an experimental disappointment? And what was so special about #2s? Were they so successful there was no need to try out the #3? Or did writing utensil connoisseurs attempt a 3 ... a 4, 5, and a 6 only to find that nothing was better than a satisfying #2?

What if Steve Jobs had created the #1? How soon would he have followed up with the #2? And would he have released the follow-up pencils in such rapid order that crowds would have camped outside Staples and Office Depot? If so, would the #5 be considered obsolete the moment purchasers walked out of the store?

I looked at the clock, stunned that thirty minutes could pass so quickly. The pencil dilemma would have to wait. Realizing my test paper was blank, I scribbled in the circles with what popped into mind. When time was up, I walked to the front of the room, dropped my paper on the corner of the desk and watched it slide across the mahogany into the teacher's hand.

Spiritual Gifts tests are graded on the spot. Had my high school teachers done that, I'd have saved a lot of money on Pepto-Bismol and Tums.

"What you'd find out?" Sue asked as she opened the car door for me.

"Tests lie," I replied keeping my eyes pointed toward my knees. "Everyone who's ever failed one knows that." I closed the door and fastened my belt, more than ready to leave.

"You can't fail it. You just ... take it," Sue reminded me. "So?"

"So?" I repeated.

"So, what'd yours say?"

"Faith." I told her. Not leadership, which I'd expected ... or wisdom, which I'd hoped for. Oh, no ... *my* spiritual gift registered as that one "thing" I doubted. That "thing" I struggled with most.

Over the next two weeks I took the test three more times, twice online and once more in a class. Yet there it was. Like glitter—the herpes of art supplies. "Faith" just wouldn't go away.

I shoved the test results—all four of them—into my desk drawer—the one that gets the least amount of attention—and went on about my life. I moved from one experience and one adventure to another. Convinced that each *good thing* that came my way was the direct result of good fortune. Not because of *faith,* mind you. Not even because of *fortitude.* All this goodness and all these blessings were flukes.

Turns out I've been focusing on the wrong F-word.

———————————

Another F-word that's registered clearly in my life: *family.* And mine is a unique one.

My mom, for instance ... has a death table.

In 1968, my great-grandmother (who was brewing coffee in the kitchen for Grampa and his brother, Elmer) was taking a bit too long. Grampa, determined to find the cause of the delay, found his mother at the kitchen table.

"It was an aneurysm," the doctors calmly told them. "It was like a light switch; she never knew what hit her."

Grampa and Elmer were born in that house, a house always full of family. With his mother's death, Elmer found himself alone there. And it stayed that way for another thirty years, at which time Grampa left a phone message for his brother. Two days passed without a return call. Determined to find the cause of the delay, Grampa went to the house. There was Elmer, in the kitchen. At that same table.

"It was an aneurysm," the doctors calmly told him. "It was like a light switch; he never knew what hit him."

As is the case whenever a family member dies, things get divvied up. Aunt Rita took the antique Philco that Grampa and Elmer had listened to World War II newsflashes and soccer matches on.

My mom took ... the table.

When my Grampa passed away—"like a light switch"—it wasn't at the table. But since this aneurism thing ran in the family, Mom's piece of furniture was now a topic of great conversation.

"A light switch, huh?" everyone asks, plopping themselves down at the four-legged wooden family heirloom. They sit before it, close their eyes, and wait. As if some mysterious flash of light or thunderous bolt of lightning will, without warning, befall them.

"You're all out of your tree!" I say, laughing and shaking my head in feigned contempt. But, as soon as they leave the room, I sit at the table and carefully look around, then close my eyes.

You know, just to make sure.

Nowadays, mom drinks coffee at that table. We eat Thanksgiving dinner at it. We talk about Grampa, Elmer, and a great-grandmother I never had the pleasure to meet. We tell stories, remember good times, and laugh for hours.

On paper it should register impossible for me to experience all the things I tell about in this book. Everything was stacked against me. An only child raised by a single mom who spent half a lifetime looking for that 25th hour of the day to make life better for us. Taking night classes here and there with occasional waitressing gigs in the afternoons.

Money (what little existed) went out faster than it came in. But in between school and restaurant jobs, mom always took to resilient measures to get more: teaching tennis in the mornings, tutoring students at night, and writing articles on the weekends for small community newspapers.

Despite being mechanically challenged in nearly every way, mom made her case to the automotive department at Sears, where she applied for a job repairing lawnmowers.

I couldn't remember her ever *pushing* a mower, much less taking one apart. Nonetheless, someone there bought her story and offered her a position on the spot. That night, she told me about the job over dinner, or "supper" as it was called back then. Mentioning it as an after thought. Like a box had just been checked midway down her list, and now it was time to move on to the pesky empty squares that still remained.

Once, when things got really bad, mom had an idea to paint ocean scenes on quartz stones. Then she combed the beach for shark teeth, bringing them home to make jewelry, selling the stones and necklaces on consignment to T-Shirt shops. Her plan worked. We had something for supper every night that summer.

My athletically inclined Mom took her mechanically innovative and entrepreneurial artistic skills on the road. At my thirteenth birthday party, a new friend asked me how many places mom and I had lived. I had to use my toes to count the number of cities. By my last year of high school, "home" had been over thirty houses, apartments, basements, townhomes, condos and "friends' places." I never spent more than three years at the same school.

Every day growing up, I balanced along a thin line of potential disasters that should have kept me down. But *faith* is what got me through it. Sometimes the faith of my mom. Sometimes my own, even when I thought I had none.

Which brings me back to that table.

Death is a part of life. And that death table is now the center of life for our family. It's become a symbol of the ultimate optimistic turn: not just the ability of taking something bad and making something good. But having the faith to realize that it will all work out in the end. Whatever "it" is.

The day my mom received her doctorate was the day that made sense to me.

It may sound a bit aberrant. But if you think that, you've missed the point entirely ... that one can find meaningful and inspirational stories even from something as unassuming as a table.

And, if carefully put together pieces of lumber can do it, then so can I.

Here are some of mine ...

Dan Beckmann

CHAPTER 1

Bush, Brokaw, and Burglary at 39,000 Feet

"I have to say that flying on Air Force One sort of spoils you for coach on a regular airline."

—Ronald Reagan

I n the fall of 2004, President George W. Bush decided to make one last campaign swing through Florida. The political landscape of the country appeared to be evenly split between "red" states and "blue" ones. Democratic challenger John Kerry had been campaigning hard for Florida's twenty-seven electoral votes, and recent polling had shown the Massachusetts senator making some headway. The political pundits colored Florida "purple." Meaning, that with just weeks before November's election, the state was still up for grabs. After the recount debacle of 2000, all eyes were on the Sunshine State. No one was anxious to see hanging or dimpled chads ever again.

Tom Brokaw had recently announced his intention to leave the anchor desk of NBC Nightly News and was pursuing long-formatted stories for the network. Recognizing Florida as a "battleground state" for the upcoming election, Mr. Brokaw decided to put together a chronicled day-to-day story on last-minute campaign strategy. The White House accepted Brokaw's request, not only offering NBC time with President Bush, but seats on Air Force One. As a cameraman for NBC, I was booked to cover the flight.

In all my time with the network, I was never quite able to understand exactly how the desk assigned crews to various stories. Obviously, correspondents had their favorite cameramen, and some crews had long standing relationships with certain producers. I was with George Bush in 2000 when I spent a few months covering his campaign on his plane with correspondent Ashleigh Banfield. But I had never worked with Tom and had never even seen Air Force One, other than on television and in pictures. With such a coup being offered, my guess was that everyone else must have been committed or on holiday. Either way, Secret Service had my information, ran my background check, and cleared me for flight with the president. After a day of appearances, we would leave from Orlando International Airport, flying south to Miami.

The Peabody Hotel in Orlando was one of the president's favorite places to stay. Why, I'm not sure. Maybe it was the ducks that lived in the Peabody penthouse and loitered around the lobby fountain all day. Maybe it was the 4.5-star rating. Or that it's so close to the tourist attractions Orlando is so famous for. I don't know. Didn't ask and he didn't offer an explanation.

The motorcade was scheduled to leave the Peabody at 5:11 a.m. Air Force One was to be "wheels up," exactly fifty-one minutes later at 6:02. Everything was timed to the second. Lucky me, with such an early call and tight window, I was allowed to stay overnight at the hotel with the White House staff.

On any normal day, traipsing through the lobby of the Peabody meant nothing more than walking through the revolving glass doors, trying your best not to get your luggage snagged in the rotating doorway behind. But this was no ordinary day. The president had already checked in and was upstairs in his room—a suite, I'm told, far less accommodating than the one those ducks lived in.

I arrived in the lobby the night before to find the familiar glass doors locked shut. Everyone entered through a single metal detector. Each person waved over with an electronic wand by men in dark suits and glasses, who talked into their sleeves every few minutes or so. They checked names and IDs on a wooden clipboard with a presidential seal emblazoned on the back. Everything was formal and ceremonious.

The hotel was crowded, but not with tourists. Everywhere I looked I saw people dressed in expensive suits boasting White House badges, with multi-colored credentials dangling from lanyards allowing each of them access to someplace important. Some places, I guessed, that didn't "officially" even exist. National correspondents from major publications pounded away on their laptops, lounging on couches tucked into quiet corners. A myriad of political conversations filled the lobby. All around were personal stories of shaking hands with world leaders and travels to faraway, exotic locales.

Once I had been cleared, I went to stand near the bar so as to have a better bead on all the chaos. Sensing someone take the seat next to me, I turned. National Security Advisor Condolezza Rice settled in mere inches from my shoulder.

Reaching for the bowl of peanuts, our hands crashed into each other. "Oh," I said. "I'm sorry, Doctor …" I fumbled for the right title. "I mean, um. Ma'am … Director."

Just as I was about to blurt out, "Your Majesty," Secretary Rice calmly pushed the bowl in my direction. I knew she'd negotiated far more difficult conflicts. This one was easy to resolve, and she yielded the next move to me.

Clearly, I was out of my element. But there I was—mixing and mingling with those closest to the President of the United States.

At ten past five the following morning, the motorcade moved out. Normally, traveling the Beeline Expressway to the airport, at any time of day, is nothing short of anarchic. Cars weaving between lanes, brake lights coming on and off again, and traffic backed up at tollbooths by drivers searching for proper change. On this morning, the road was as quiet as a church mouse, save for the sirens of the police cars and motorcycles that led the presidential motorcade to the airport.

Air Force One is big – all 4,000 square feet of interior floor space. I noticed the plane parked on the tarmac next to a hanger built to accommodate large commercial aircraft. It was too large to be parked inside.

As the morning sun peeked just above the tree line at the end of the runway, I began another round of clearances. Inching closer to the plane, I passed through another metal detector and was given one final wand search and a last clipboard check at the base of a stairway, which led to an opened hatch door bearing the presidential seal.

I was aboard Air Force One. Everyone on the plane seemed to know his or her destination, except my audio operator Mike Huntting, and me. I looked at Mike like a deer stares into headlights. His wide-eyed glance confirmed we were in perfect harmony. It wasn't so much that we didn't know where to go. We didn't. But, more importantly, Mike and I realized *we were on Air Force One*. We were waiting for *Tom Brokaw*, so we could hang out with *the President of the United States of America*.

We settled into comfortable leather chairs, facing each other with more legroom than first-class accommodations on a commercial aircraft. My seat had its own window and on every armrest was a box of M&M's with the presidential seal. Looking out my window, I noticed the president's limo parked just under the wing of the aircraft. Brokaw was walking from it, stopping at the clipboard checkpoint Mike and I had cleared minutes earlier.

Tom arrived with a White House official, and we were ushered into an adjacent conference room to wait for the president. The interview, we were told, could last no more than six minutes. Mr. Bush was on a tight schedule. With nothing to do but wait, we sat, unsupervised, in a room on the most sophisticated airplane ever built, waiting for the most powerful man in the world.

Mike and I had brought very little equipment—a camera of course, audio gear, and a backpack, which contained a few extra batteries.

I started making a mental checklist of the situation: A) I was on Air Force One; B) I had lots of room in my backpack; C) There were many cool things on the airplane; and D) No one was watching me. In some so-crazy-I-can't-believe-I-even-thought-this moment, I decided that whatever could fit into my backpack was going home with me.

First, I eased my hand up to my head, pretending to scratch an itch I didn't have … then I swiped the headrest cover off the Velcro "securing" it place. Next up, the little boxes of M&M's. Walking past the rows of seats I covertly snatched every box, propelling each one into my bag. Those things are never packed to the brim so, thinking the rattling candy might give me away I shoved tissue paper on top of the sweets to keep the noise at a minimum. Then snatched the entire *box* of Kleenex.

In a normal bathroom, there isn't much to take notice of. But in the lavatories on Air Force One, a treasure chest of items goaded my thievery. A toothbrush with the presidential seal on the handle was an easy item to conceal. Harder to hide—but not impossible—was the water glass with a bald eagle etched into the base.

Even the toilet paper was first-rate. It must have been thirty-ply because it felt thick enough to dry off after a shower. There wasn't a seal to be found anywhere on it, so I left it hanging on the roller.

I took Tic Tacs, a box of soap, hand sanitizer, and a white washcloth with a bright blue Air Force One logo stitched along the bottom. I plopped myself upon the toilet seat cover, thinking surely someone important had sat in the same spot at some point.

Just outside the bathroom, a beautiful, hand-carved coaster was strategically placed on the conference room table. Inscribed into its base was another presidential emblem. I tried in vain to free it, but it must have been super-glued in place. After a failed attempt at prying it off, I caught sight of a shiny, stainless steel, presidential seatbelt buckle. It was the most beautiful emblazoned buckle I'd ever seen. But it had apparently been crafted by the same individual who made the coaster, because that thing wasn't going *anywhere* either.

More determined than ever to possess what I could not have, I came up with a foolproof plan. But, just as I was about to gnaw it off the strap, the President of the United States entered the room. I had to put my delinquent behavior on hold and get to work.

President Bush sat at the head of the table and, after a few moments of idle chitchat, the interview began. Brokaw asked the president about the political mapping of the country, why Florida was important, and if he felt his chances for a second term in the Oval Office looked good. President Bush answered in that oh-so-casual way he has of speaking and, six minutes later, we were done. Putting the camera on the floor then standing, as protocol would dictate, I waited for the president to make his exit. Mike stood as well. But President Bush didn't move. Relaxed as could be, still sitting in his chair, he continued talking with Tom. It was mundane chatter, really. Celebrities that got under his skin, baseball teams he thought would have a good season the following year. A White House staffer motioned for me to sit down. It was pretty clear the president didn't feel like leaving.

Mike and I found ourselves sitting at a table with one of the most respected and renowned TV journalists in history, *and* the President of the United States, not to mention a bagful of stolen Air Force One items at my feet.

Ten minutes later, a knock at the door and the First Lady stepped in. She'd decided to say "hello" to Tom. Instead of a quick meet-and-greet, Laura Bush took the open chair next to her husband. Not long after Mrs. Bush's arrival, there was another knock. This time, Condoleeza Rice came in. The conversation switched to football.

The room was growing with people. Bush and Brokaw talked baseball, the first lady spoke about the poor conditions of public schools, and Condoleeza discussed the NFL. And, while I should have been *kvelling* at having reached such a moment in my career, all I could think about was how to get off the plane before being charged with a dozen federal crimes of theft and piracy.

I stole one last thing: a look at Mike. In silent acknowledgement we decided to slink ever closer to the back wall, lest we be found out for even *being* in the room!

Before anyone had time to slap handcuffs on my wrists, we landed in Miami and right on time. After a few campaign stops and a couple of motorcade drives through the city, the president and Air Force One flew back to D.C.

But without me.

I was on my way to Miami International from where I would fly home … in coach.

Looking out the window, my body pinned against the seat, I watched the shadow of the wing disappear from the runway as that floating sensation rolled in my stomach. It was a much bumpier takeoff than Air Force One. That's when I thought of all the things I'd done. Not just that morning or the night before, but rather how I'd even gotten to this moment in the first place. How a kid like me, who grew up in one small city after another, *ever* managed to find himself flying on Air Force One with the President of the United States. No one back home would ever believe it. I'd just lived it and I couldn't quite take it all in. But it happened. As had a number of other things. Remarkable things. Fantastic and wondrous things that, as a kid, I only *dreamed* possible.

Reaching into my backpack, I pulled out one of the M&M boxes. I opened it and popped a couple into my mouth. Dreaming of my next adventure, I realized each tasted like every other M&M I'd ever had. But I was keeping the box.

No question about that.

CHAPTER 2

Music in the Midwest: The Sound of My Formidable Years

"Music was my refuge. I could crawl into the space between the notes and curl my back to loneliness."

—Maya Angelou

The most impressionable period of my life—or, at least, according to the majority of psychologists and psychiatrists what *should have been* the most impressionable period of my life—took place in a modest house on Stillbrook Estates Drive in Fenton, Missouri.

Fenton, a small suburb thirty-minutes southwest of St. Louis, was as middle America as you could get, both in geography and status. Stillbrook was a newly built middle-class subdivision, which sat at the top of a lonely hill. And what seemed idyllic at first glance, upon closer inspection was tinged with troublesome issues. Two red-bricked, low-rent apartment buildings flanked the entrance. And, if that didn't shrink the property value of the new homes, Shangri-La, the disjointed clumps of broken-down doublewides that encompassed nearly all the land in the valley below, certainly did.

Like the scintillating shine of a new car, every home on our street had a pristine appearance and each lined up smartly alongside the next, dotting the single road that made up our neighborhood. Landscaping, though, took a backseat. Patchy remnants of sod, weeds, and construction debris littered each yard.

Every house looked just like the next. Except for an occasional front door placed on the opposite side of the garage, confusing the eye and making them appear slightly different.

On the other hand, Shangri-La was unruly. A prison yard without walls. I imagined trigger-happy guards daring to hurl buckshot at anyone who dared an escape. It was always difficult to recognize firecrackers from live fire.

Each night, the sound of street fights and arguments from the trailers below traveled up the hill, spilling onto our dinner tables. Causing our fathers to square their shoulders, our mothers to purse their lips, and us Stillbrook kids to wonder what was really going on "down there."

"Down there" was home to some of the meanest kids I'd ever seen. Most of them were backwoods delinquents who spelled school with a "K." They spent the better part of their days setting fire to small woodland creatures with a magnifying glass and their nights planning what they'd do to us fortunate ones who lived up the hill.

We were sure of it.

Zeke was their leader. He didn't have a last name. In fact, I don't think he even had parents. If he did, he probably ate them. Zeke was our residential Goliath, standing at what seemed like eight-foot tall. Rumor had it he consumed chickens whole and served years in juvenile detention for bludgeoning his entire class with a breadbox he made in shop class. It was a reputation he relished.

As a teenager, a reputation is important. In our neighborhood, it defined us. And the kind of music we listened to determined our place in the pecking order of our adolescent hierarchy. Zeke liked Black Sabbath, so he pretty much scared *everyone* into submission. For the rest of us, listening to Boston or Blue Oyster Cult meant you were cool. Get caught listening to Lionel Ritchie and you were sure to become a social eunuch.

My mom had been my only conduit to music. Luckily for me, she played it all the time. Not so lucky was her taste. She wore out the needle on our record player listening to Carol King's *Tapestry* and Captain and Tennille's *Love Will Keep Us Together*. One day, she brought home an album by Culture Club.

"I've got a crush on that girl," I told her.

"What girl?" she asked, looking a little worried.

"The one on the cover," I said, pointing to Boy George.

Her expression changed from worried to weird.

I had no idea how much she was screwing me up.

One morning, an imposing kid from the trailer park came up to me at the bus stop. He had long, oily black hair, wore dirty pants, and always had on the same ripped-up blue jean jacket with a large skull patch on the back. He was one of Zeke's underlings, a truant aficionado who had never given me so much as the time of day. Although I wasn't convinced he could even tell time, he scared me to death. I avoided him like my homework assignments. Once, he looked in my direction, terrifying me so much that I ran, tipping chairs behind me to slow an impending pursuit. But now he was walking up *to* me. And he was opening his mouth. Talking.

"You like Jethro Tull?" he asked.

Okay. So not only was he walking up to me and talking to me, *now* he was asking me a question. A question he obviously expected an answer to.

Think, Danny, think!

Standing in puddles of my own sweat, I looked for a place to throw up. Thoughts, one on top of the other, racing through my mind:

"Do I have or need a will?"

"Does my mom know I love her?"

"Was it actually possible to snap a human in half?"

I had to do something. Something fast. Not that I wanted to be his friend, but it was so much better than being his enemy.

"Well, do you or don't you?" he asked again.

I cleared my throat. Shifted from one foot to the other and back again. "Jethro?" I said, the answer coming out in a squeak. Someone pull the fire alarm! Pull it *now*! I cleared my throat again. Forced my voice to go lower. "Of course, I do. Who doesn't?"

"Good," he replied. He towered over me, coolly smacking a pack of cigarettes into the palm of his hand. A single one shot out like a stiletto. It was a thing of beauty. Clearly, he'd done this many times. I watched, in reverence, as he lit up while we waited for the bus.

I looked around. There was no blood on me anywhere. I was still alive.

"Want a smoke?" he asked, taking another out from behind his ear and handing it to me.

I held out my hands as if taking communion, remembering something about a surgeon general and absolute death. I'd never smoked before. Didn't even know how. But we had cable and I was pretty sure I remembered the modus operandi from a movie I'd once seen.

1. *Grab cigarette with index finger and thumb of left hand.*
2. *Insert into mouth.*
3. *Flip metal thingy to make a flame with right hand.*
4. *Put fire on tip of cigarette while cupping left hand over flame.*
5. *Breathe in.*

"Wait …" I said, staring at this kid's gift resting in the palm of my hand. "Which end goes into the mouth again?"

He didn't say a word. Not one. But his sneer spoke plenty. My one moment of coolness … far too fleeting. Unless …

"Hey!" I said quickly. "You know who's better than Jethro?"

"Who?" he asked, his dark eyes sizing me up and down.

"Ellie Mae," I said. "Now she's *hot*!"

I wasn't sure what I'd said but, from the look on his face, I was about to be pulverized. Just then, a not-too-distant rumble turned his attention away from his part in my pummeling. The bus made an early arrival.

He looked from the bus, then back at me. With an unwavering gaze of disgust normally reserved for a bug about to be dispatched, he flicked his cigarette and ground it out on the top of my shoe. The doors swung open, he pushed me aside, got on first, and went straight to the back with all the other criminals. I sat near the front, next to a kid with thick, black-framed Buddy Holly glasses and a bright green Izod. His hair was parted down the middle with what smelled like Vicks Vapor Rub. He was a walking birth-control device, but it was the only open seat.

"You ever watch the Beverly Hillbillies? You know, the show with Ellie Mae?" I asked, as the bus began to roll.

"Sure. Yeah," he replied. I could tell he had no idea where this was going.

"Jethro Tull …" I said. "That's her brother, right?"

Without saying a word, he stepped over me and crammed himself into a seat next to two kids who were actively engaged in smearing the contents of their noses on the window. With half his butt cheek hanging in the aisle, I heard him mumble the word "microphallus" under his breath as he shook his head in disgust.

Thinking I could look it up if only I knew how to spell it, I realized there and then, in the gene pool of our community, I was lower than the biggest geek in school.

Getting my Jethros mixed up forced me to get serious about music. I fired my mom and hired MTV. While the other kids hated pop music, I secretly reveled in it. I knew every word to Wham's *Wake Me Up Before You Go Go,* and I thought Banarama's *Cruel Summer* was catchy and fun. And if word of that *ever* spread to my classmates, I'd have had third-degree Indian burns and endless wedgies that would last until graduation. So I kept my TV at low volume. Even outside walls were paper thin, and I didn't need any more musical misfires.

My biggest concern as a teenager wasn't acne, braces, or finding a date to the prom. It was Starship. First of all, they kept changing their name and I had no one to discuss it with. Secondly, and even more important, their latest hit, *We Built This City,* was so terrible and had saturated itself into my brain so deeply, I feared I'd be overheard accidentally humming it. If caught, I'd immediately disappear into an unmarked locker, setting off a chain of events that would cast my demise into the annals of urban legend.

One afternoon, Zeke trudged up the hill to our street in clear violation of the Peace Treaty. Without saying a word, he punched me square in the face then stood to admire his handiwork. Within seconds, my mom emerged. Bolting from the front door, darting in my direction, she mummified my head with ripped pieces of towel we used, typically on Saturdays, to clean the car. A bit excessive for a bloodied nose, but at least she scared off Zeke before he finished the job.

To this day, I don't know what precipitated the attack. Perhaps he'd heard of the Beverly Hillbillies debacle or maybe caught wind of me singing REO Speedwagon's *Can't Fight This Feeling* the night before. Could I have been so careless to have left the window cracked? It may, quite simply, have been his way of maintaining quality control.

Regardless, I felt I deserved the punishment. Clearly I'd mishandled the Jethro Tull incident, and those songs I learned from MTV really weren't helping.

Aside from the occasional pubescent skirmish and the sometimes breaching of the Peace Treaty, our little street was fairly safe and quite comfortable. There was often a neighborhood block party going on, and we all looked out for one another as best we could. We were more than happy to have a roof over our heads. And if we wanted for anything, we didn't know what it was. It was easier not knowing how the "upper half" lived.

During long summer nights and on pleasant weekday afternoons, I played catch in Jimmy Sealy's driveway. That is, until Shawn Anders' dad put a fence up in their backyard. After that, playing over at Shawn's was like playing in our own little stadium. The chain link enclosure made hitting home runs official.

Jimmy, Shawn, and I were inseparable. In the summers, we'd take turns spending the night at whomever's parents could handle the late-night laughs and crude, adolescent jokes. It was our life's ambition to stay up a full twenty-four hours. We never made it.

The only future we knew was the afternoon. We shot bottle rockets at one another from the end of our whiffle-ball bats. When the projectiles ran out, we made dirt clots and threw those at each another. Moving on to mailboxes before nightfall, eviscerating them with ninja swords we made from tree branches. The three of us were always having fun. It just never dawned on us we were doing it wrong.

No matter what we were doing though, we stopped doing it the moment we heard the sound of the ice cream truck. Our mother's voices calling us for dinner from only a few yards away were never audible. Yet, somehow, we could discern the chimes of that soft-serve mobile retail outlet playing *It's a small world (after all)* from the next state over.

Winters meant snow. And for Jimmy, Shawn, and me that meant money. We pushed stranded cars up the slippery hill and onto the top of our street. By day's end, we had enough cash to buy entire boxes of baseball cards and time to flip through them over a large pepperoni pizza in downtown Fenton.

Dave Krigby was sixteen, lived next door, and had a car. For three slices, he'd drive us into town. We'd meet him at the top of the hill and around the corner of the apartment buildings so no one would see us get in.

"Fenton's small. And I've got a reputation to maintain," Dave would say.

We'd jump in, quickly and covertly, so as not to attract attention.

"Keep your heads down!" Dave would command. We'd drive into town, the three of us tightly bunched in cannonball positions on the floor of his car.

It was all very clandestine and, in fact, ridiculous. I was never quite sure what reputation Dave envisioned himself having, seeing as how we were slouched in a dented, brown, 1964 Dodge Dart that only seemed to start on Tuesdays and Thursdays. Dave's front seats were falling apart and springs popped through the cracked vinyl allowing for un-intentional prostate exams if you sat at the just the wrong position. The car had but one wiper blade and it squeaked smearing wet dirt across the windshield whenever it rained. Dave had wrenched the other one off to use as a dipstick for the oil. The interior roof was tattered and worn with chunks of foam falling off every time he hit a bump in the road. His car always smelled like dirty feet; to lower the window you had to use pliers because the passenger-side handle had fallen off years earlier.

Dave's car was a junkyard on wheels and his own appearance matched it perfectly. His hair was habitually disheveled, and it looked as though he'd gotten all of his clothes from the wardrobe department of a 70's sitcom. He had one pair of pants, a thick, cottony-fabric kind with velvety ribs.

"They're called corduroy," he said proudly. "Everybody's wearing them."

Dave was portly and his waist spilled over his belt, forcing him to wrap a piece of shirt around his buckle, so as not to pinch any skin. He was a life-sized Weeble-Wobble who reeked of smoke—a funny kind of smoke—and he was always coming up with new ways to get dates. At least in theory … we never actually saw him with any girls. Perhaps dorkier than anyone on the block, still, he was the only kid with a driver's license who knew our names. Which made him, by default, the *coolest* guy on the block. Corduroy or not.

On my sixteenth birthday, after passing my driver's test, my grandparents presented me with a gift. As a celebration for that right-of-passage, I became the proud owner of a blue 1975 AMC Hornet. I had just been bequeathed a family treasure—the very same car my Grampa had driven off the lot, brand spanking new, just ten years before.

Later that day, I decided I was ready for my first solo drive, a quick spin through the tiny downtown of Fenton. Dave leaned in through the passenger window while I went through my checklist.

Mirror, mirroring.

Seat belt, belting.

Wipers, wiping. (Both of them.)

And most important, radio, radioing.

USA for Africa's, *We Are the World* came on. I sang along.

"You can't do that!" Dave said, reaching for the knob and turning the radio off.

"What's the matter?" I asked.

"Are you kidding me?" he said. "Shangri-La hears that coming out of your car, and there go your tires."

"Here … try this," he said, handing me a cassette of REM songs. I popped it in and got lost in the words of *Fall On Me*.

Suddenly, I found myself in a different world. I was growing musically *and* I was mobile. Playing in the street was a part of my past. And, as unsightly as it looked, that AMC Hornet was the fuel of my future. I didn't know where I was going but, wherever it was, I had a car that could take me there. And Jimmy and Shawn didn't. The day the two of them fought over who was more talented, Debbie Gibson or Tiffany, I thought it was time to put them in my rearview mirror.

And to think I had managed to keep the entire Starship situation to myself.

Dave's car may have rarely started, but the battery always worked. One typical spring evening, which was the only comfortable time of the year seasonally, I found myself sitting with Dave in his front seat, listening to music on his new stereo.

"It cost more than the car," he said.

I wanted to tell him the knobs probably cost more too, but thought better of it. Dave had replaced MTV in my life and was fast becoming a brilliant tutor. I wanted to graduate with my teeth, so I kept my mouth shut.

He introduced me to Lynard Skynard.

I introduced him to Madonna.

I was a slow learner.

"You bring that crap in this car one more time," he said, pointing a finger inches from my nose, "and you can find yourself another friend." He was serious.

We discussed important issues, like the evolution of Bowie's androgyny and which girl from Heart was better looking. I wanted to ask if Michael Jackson's red zippered jacket from Thriller would be cool to wear, but felt I might fail the exam. Instead, we dissected The Who's *Baba O'Reilly*, or *Teenage Wasteland* as I called it. And the world became different.

Everything started to make perfect sense. Until Dave put on Pink Floyd.

"You know. If you start *Dark Side of the Moon* at the same time as *The Wizard of Oz*, the two match up perfectly," he said, in a monotone voice.

"Really?" I asked. "How exactly does that work?"

"I don't know, man. I don't know," he said. "But you have to wait until after the MGM lion roars the third time." He shook his head and closed his eyes. Like churning butter, I cranked the pliers and lowered the window to let the funny smelling smoke melt into the outside air.

One afternoon, while arguing over whether or not The Police "sold out" with the release of *Zenyatta Mondatta*, Dave mentioned a Six Flags job fair he'd heard was underway at the Holiday Inn just up the road.

"If our cars can't get us dates, maybe a bit of cash in our pockets can," Dave said, as he put his key in the ignition. For a brief, shining moment, he sounded excited about what lay ahead.

He turned the key. Nothing. Not a sound.

He flashed me the most pitiful of expressions. "It's Wednesday," I said. "What'd you expect? I'll drive."

Dave and I were hired on the spot and told to report in two weeks time.

On our first day, we were introduced to Jeremy, an eighteen-year-old supervisor who ran the food service/dishwashing department.

Jeremy had been working at Six Flags since he was fifteen and believed he was born to be a culinary/business mastermind. He was tall and gangly and wore shirts that buttoned all the way up. His pants had creases down the front that could cut diamonds but were never quite long enough. Jeremy had an Adam's apple that stuck out far enough for a bird to perch on. His hair was always cut short, never out of place. And his pocket protector bulged with an assortment of pens for every occasion and writing surface.

I was convinced he was the president of his high school chess club. And he, most likely, paid dearly for that with the other kids. For some reason, he took a liking to me and began dispersing advice on a regular basis.

"With a little hard work," he said, "you'll make Line Leader by the time you're thirty!"

He didn't feel the same about Dave. Jeremy had some strange notion that Dave should only come to work sober. But Dave was always too stoned to grasp that logic. After a few ego-bruising altercations, Dave quit.

Not too long after we began our Six Flags employment experience and even more shortly after Dave left for a vocation/vacation unknown, Jeremy moved me to the coveted Employee Food Line. It seemed there was no one better at ladling just the right amount of gravy over the instant flakes of mashed potatoes than me. I was, as he said, "On the fast track to managerial prominence."

After a month, my dreams of stardom faded with each semi-solid substance I threw on the plates. The clock ticked by oh-so-slowly … slowly … slowly. Tick. Tick. Tick. I grew tired of smelling like beans and tacos at the end of each shift. But I made the best of my fast food festivities, becoming a self-appointed and self-trained food line performance artist. I scooped the broccoli from behind my back, and dunked fallen pieces of meat into the trash from ten feet away.

One afternoon—while making magic with the macaroni and daydreaming about Tawny Kittan cart wheeling over the hood of my Hornet—Nancy Thornburg, Six Flags' Manager of Entertainment, snapped me to attention with her Coke order. A former background dancer for Salt-n-Pepa (or maybe it was Poison; I often got my girl bands and hair bands confused), Nancy was nearly forty to my almost seventeen. She was barely a hundred pounds; had pretty, long black hair, and the brownest eyes I'd ever seen. She had a body that resembled a brick wall and a handshake like a vice. She could have broken me in two with her index finger. Ellie Mae had nothing on her!

Nancy told me she was in charge of all the shows, dancers, and costumed characters, such as Daffy Duck and Yosemite Sam. Unfazed by the line backing up through the door and spilling onto the sidewalk, she kept talking.

"You know," Nancy said inquisitively, drumming her fingers on the counter. "I'm thinking Bugs."

"What?" I said, petrified, looking in all directions. "Where are they?" I asked in a whisper. "Are they in the salad again? I sprayed last night. I swear!"

"Not *bugs*. Bugs Bunny," she said. "*That rascally rabbit …*" She waved her arms, cut a jig on the linoleum, and sang, "*Overture, curtains, lights …*"

Before the patient folks waiting for their food turned ugly, I rushed from my side to her side of the serving area. "Yeah, yeah. Okay. I know what you mean. The rabbit. Gotcha," I said, putting her arms back to her sides for her.

She reached for a nearby napkin dispenser, pulled one sheet of thin paper free. "Here," she said, scribbling her phone number on it. "Don't lose this. Call me." She winked up at me. "We'll have a good time."

"Okay," I said, putting the napkin in my pocket. I went back to my position behind the counter and handed her a soda. Nancy poked a straw in her drink, gave me another wink, and then turned to leave, revealing a smiling kid—thirteen if he was a day—next in line.

"Older women," he said, nodding in approval. "Nice job!"

The next day, I was off the food line and assigned to "Entertainment."

The following week was spent watching Looney Tunes, copying the moves, imitating character mannerisms, and learning to walk in oversized clown shoes that made running impossible. I was getting *paid* to watch cartoons. Something I never dreamed possible. Ronald Reagan could *have* the presidency. *This* was the best job in the world.

Or so I thought.

The guests mostly smiled as I greeted them into the park each day. But every now and then some kid would absolutely lose his mind, screaming, horrified, as he caught sight of a giant rabbit bounding from around a corner. I never took that personally. While I was bringing to life America's most beloved bunny, to that little crying kid, I was a tall hairy creature coming to eat him.

Another drawback to being a character was the heat. Summers in St. Louis could be stifling. Even hotter than being greased and lying out by a pool was being inside a furry costume that consumed the entire body. After our first one-hundred-degree day, Nancy instituted the 30/30 Rule. Thirty minutes in the park followed immediately by a half hour of "down time" in our Green Room, better known as "The Pit."

Having only thirty minutes in The Pit meant getting completely out of costume wasn't possible. It took too long to get our enormous feet Velcro-strapped in place, our paws secured, and our fur brushed. So we grew accustomed to throwing off our heads, unzipping halfway, and falling onto the floor beneath the whir of the fans. Downing ice-cold water so quickly we'd get a brain freeze the moment it hit our teeth.

Yes, gone were the smells of tacos and re-fried beans. But, after one shift in the St. Louis sun, entirely new aromas arose. Lysol cans were our best friends.

For two summers I dressed as a rabbit and, occasionally, as Wiley Coyote. I made a lot of friends, dated Daffy Duck and had a ball. But even at seventeen, I knew there was no future as a Looney Tune. I had hit the glass ceiling of costumed entertainers.

Working at Six Flags taught me something it would take me years to fully understand: each step we take in life is but a stepping-stone in preparation for the next. Learning to walk in Bugs Bunny feet was not easy, but it prepared me for my next challenge: marching in formation. The record of my youth was about to flip to the B Side.

CHAPTER 3

Stars, Stripes, and *Yikes*!

"Draft beer. Not people."

—**Unknown**

From the Midwest to MCRD

Two guiding forces directed me to the United States military. The first was my desire to emulate Tom Cruise's character Maverick from the movie *Top Gun*. The second, and more realistic, was my mom's decision and determination to find someone other than *her* to be legally responsible for the hellion I'd become.

At seventeen, I was too young to join on my own. So my mother—more than a little disappointed that the draft was no longer *enforceable*—literally snatched the papers from my recruiter's hands. "Just ... show me ... where to sign the thing." Her words interrupted the recruiter explaining what a four-year commitment meant.

Seeing what could have easily been perceived as "backing out" written all over my face and sheer terror in my eyes, the recruiter spoke up. "Hey, …" he said, with a snap of his fingers. "It'll go by like *that*."

The look on Mom's face told me it wasn't *nearly* long enough.

I was about to shake my head and say, "No thank you," when the recruiter mentioned something about "seeing the world," something I'd always wanted to do. While the man's words painted pictures, I envisioned myself relaxing on the beaches of Greece, climbing to the top of Kilimanjaro, and sailing in the Mediterranean. Little did I know his idea of the "world" was the Mojave Desert, classified areas in Nevada, and the hotter-than-hell missile facility near Charleston, South Carolina; a swampy state where mosquitoes were only slightly smaller than Frisbees, roaches sprouted wings and No-see-ums came as unintentional appetizers before meals.

I found myself on an airplane a mere eight days after gripping my diploma in one hand and the high school principal's with the other. Along with a dozen other new recruits, I was on my way to boot camp, leaving behind the boring Midwest for the excitement of Southern California. Behind me was the Bowling Hall of Fame. Just ahead—or so my recruiter told me—were endless sandy white beaches where women frolicked in bikinis and played volleyball near the dunes. He'd also mentioned something about living in spacious condominiums. I had no trouble whatsoever picturing exactly what mine would look like. Cool glass and chrome furniture, leather sofas and a wet bar in the corner. I was embarking toward one long party.

I had never been west of the Mississippi, and the only time I'd been on an airplane was to visit my grandparents for the summer. That was a sixty-minute ride when I was nine. This flight was over three hours and our plane was nearly empty. Except for us recruits and a few accountants on their way to a tax convention.

"It's all about the deductible," Gerald, one of the accountants, told me. "You see, you take the standard deduction, ..." he droned on and on for what seemed liked days—his dull cadence putting me in a hypnotic state.

Tony, a recruit from Indiana, leaned over and whispered in my ear ... "Ten bucks says ten weeks of military training is way better than his three-day event."

"I'm not taking that bet," I said through the corner of my mouth.

"So brave!" Lola the flight attendant sighed, squeezing my shoulder with one hand and handing me a soda with the other. Her expression seemed far too concerned for my liking. Obviously she hadn't heard about the white sandy beaches...the girls in bikinis...the volleyball tournaments.

It wasn't until the captain announced our descent, telling us recruits to enjoy the last bit of freedom we were going to experience for a while, that I began to understand the reason for her worried looks.

We touched down in California a little before three in the morning. The plane taxied to a halt, and Lola opened a door that led us down a set of rickety stairs onto the tarmac. I staggered curiously toward the terminal while the warm, dry heat enveloped every inch of me. There was no wind ... just hot, stifling, noiseless air.

This was the calm before the storm.

The moment we stepped into the bright lights of the terminal, we were accosted by a prickly old man in camouflage. His face showed years of wear, tear, and battle. He had to be ... at *least* ... thirty.

The "old man" marched us through the airport barking, "Left! Right! Left! Right!" along the way. Each of us was immeasurably out of step with the person in front, which only made him more ferocious. Everything we attempted was wrong causing him to explode periodically into fits.

Just outside the terminal, double-parked in a loading zone, was a battleship gray, cheerless old bus waiting to take us to MCRD, the Marine Corps Recruitment Depot. We boarded in a mental fog of numbness. Each of us clueless as to what was happening and too scared to inquire. Our leathery leader got on last, made a quick head count, commanded us to remain silent (no problem there), and motioned to the driver to make haste.

"Faith." was not the "F-Word" that came immediately to mind.

It was like sleepwalking with strangers—all of us heading for the same wake-up: that horrifying moment when we "snap to" and find ourselves in a strange place wondering how we got there.

We drove through the San Diego night. The bus windows only opened to slits—not nearly wide enough to make an escape—thus allowing a warm breeze to trickle in. Some time later, the screech and burst of the 21 Air-Brake Salute signaled our arrival. I had no idea how long the ride was but I knew I hadn't blinked since I left the airport.

In single file, we marched into a well-lit building, which we were told to call "barracks." Stark, brilliant lights hit us from every direction. There was a sterile cleanliness any hospital would have been proud of. Dust was too frightened to settle. The walls were polished with a smooth, dingy gray lacquer. Rows of neatly made beds stood in attention on both sides of the aisle. A constant "hum" murmured from the incandescent lights overhead and the floors had a lustrous shine that reflected our unsure images like mirrors. It was the scariest and most exhilarating moment of my life; a mixed cocktail of emotions I had never before encountered.

The buildings, desks, pens, boots, and uniforms—though effective—came from the cheapest materials, apparently made by the lowest bidder. Military barbers were no exception.

As a kid, getting a haircut at the mall was a big deal: Bruce's Wash-n-Blow being my favorite. Bruce talked funny and he walked like one of the girls from Charlie's Angels. And there was always music playing—typically disco—and mirrors festooned every inch of the walls. He had a refrigerator full of ice-cold Coca-Cola in tiny glass bottles. Coke always tastes better in glass.

"Here ya go. Try this swizzle straw. I just think it's *thee* most festive!" Bruce had a way of adding an extra "e" for emphasis. He had plush, cushiony seats and I always felt relaxed in them. He washed my hair with shampoo that smelled like peppermint and avocado or honey melon. And while he washed, I talked about matchbox cars and G.I. Joes.

Bruce talked about *Cosmo*.

"What's a *Cosmo*?" I asked him once.

"*What's a Cosmo?*" Bruce seemed completely shocked; looking at me as if I'd just stepped in something foul. "Only *thee* best magazine in *thee* whole wide world!"

Bruce's Wash N' Blow was fun. Needless to say, military barbershops are not. In fact, this barbershop didn't even have a mirror. I wasn't offered a coke, there wasn't any music, and the only conversation came from the cadence of the soldiers outside, jabbering on about some man from Nantucket.

A noisy pair of clippers never shut off. Each haircut took less than a minute; we recruits were like an assembly line of sheep being sheared in a barn. It actually required more time to sweep away the hair on the floor than it did to take it off our heads.

When it was my turn, I marched to the chair like a good soldier. "Sit!" The command was big and booming; I thought it sounded like God talking.

I adjusted myself as comfortably as possible in a most uncomfortable plastic chair.

"*Just* a smidgeon off the sides, please," I said with my usual sarcastic humor.

The barber wasn't amused.

"You got a *Cosmo* I can look at while I'm being styled?" I said, but still no response.

"How 'bout a bendy straw and a Coca-Cola?" I asked.

Nothing.

Figuring him to be about my mother's age, I thought I'd come up with the perfect connection. "No Coke? Got any Tab?"

No bonding. No nothing…just the blades of the shears running from the front to the back of my head. There was no conversation at all. Suddenly, the chair swiveled around so I was face-to-face with the barber. He darted his eyes back and forth over my head. After admiring his handy work, he lowered the clippers, signaling he was done. "Get up!" he barked. "You're good."

With a satisfactory nod, he motioned for me to retreat to the end of the line. The same line I had just gotten out of. I thought I caught a sly grin as he turned away, putting the next recruit into the chair I'd warmed up.

Two things were bothering me. One: why did I have to get back into the same line I'd just gotten out of?

Two: why was everyone laughing?

I scratched my head and got the answer to both; I had but half a mane.

I strained to get an image off the waxed floors. But I didn't really need to see. Convinced I looked like someone who trimmed their own bangs with a hacksaw after a long night of drinking, I decided this would be the last time I'd attempt to have a sense of humor during basic.

Military Purgatory

Adjacent to the barbershop was a drab concrete building we were told to call "home." Social Security Numbers, written in black Sharpie on cards taped to each set of bunks, directed us to our new and humbling abode. It was a far cry from a divan. No posters on the corners of the bed, no feathers in my pillows. Just gray frames stacked on top of one another. A hard, spring-less mattress with wrinkle-free sheets sat on wire webbing with metal fittings that secured everything in place. Every night of basic, I'd sleep suspended between sandpaper.

The view from my window provided no signs of beaches, girls in bikinis, or volleyball games. Instead, I saw miles of obstacle courses with giant rope ladders and monkey bars. It was my own private "Private Benjamin" realization. There weren't any condos.

I'd been had.

What lay in wait for me were ten weeks of morning, afternoon, and evening drills; 4:00 a.m. breakfasts, 4:00 p.m. dinners, and 6:00 p.m. "lights out." Tossed beds, grueling marches, endless pushups, and thirty-second cold showers with eighty strange-looking bald-headed guys, each of us wondering why we'd been given shampoo *and* conditioner.

Three days into boot camp, we were still nearly a dozen recruits short of a company. Until we expanded our number, we were tasked with an uninteresting amount of daily chores: dusting, shining, and washing any and every inanimate object visible to the naked eye. We were armed with a rag and a spray bottle of disinfectant. The only weapon we were allowed to carry was a toothbrush for scrubbing toilets. I learned just how well something designed for the enamel in my mouth worked to get at those hard-to-reach areas around the base of a toilet. I had signed up to be a fighting machine, but the only things afraid of me were germs and the occasional dust bunny.

One day, while we waited to form our company, we spent an afternoon in career orientation. "Choose your field specialty wisely," our company commander told us. "You're gonna be stuck with it."

And with that impassioned counsel, we were ushered into a room and told to take a seat.

Within minutes, a woman—a civilian—in a white dress and paper nurse's hat entered the room. "Stand by and wait for your name to be called," she said. Her voice was calm. Soothing. Her glasses were inches thick. Feet so large the laces of her shoes were disintegrating into threads. She had teeth that reminded me of a Jack-o-lantern. Still, she was the first woman I'd seen in weeks, which made her *really hot.*

The testosterone poison had nearly done me in. I'd been spending twenty-four hours a day with several dozen guys in close proximity. Everywhere I turned there was another five o'clock shadow, another sweat stain. Burping. Belching. Snorting. And scratching. Things oozing from orifices no one should ever have to be subjected to. Yet here I was, surrounded by all of it with no way out.

The lady with big feet and shredded shoelaces could have been a Sasquatch. But the fact that she was carrying ovaries and mammary glands made her irresistible.

When she called my name, I rose to attention — literally and figuratively.

"Follow me," she said, in that intoxicatingly sultry voice. Excited to finally be inches from the opposite sex, I obeyed. I closed my eyes and breathed her in. She smelled like a hospital. Yet, somehow, she radiated electric code and pheromones.

She motioned for me to sit in a chair across from a man in dress whites with shoulder boards. He was an officer. The first one I'd ever seen.

"Sooooooo…" he began, turning a one-syllable word into four. "What is it you're interested in doing?"

"Well," I said. "I dunno exactly. I think I wanna fly planes or be a doctor."

The officer glanced up from the yellow, coffee-stained legal pad where he'd been scribbling notes with all the excitement of a turtle in a hare race.

"Okay. You know you need a college degree for those, right?" He shoved his notebook aside.

"Oh, yeah. Sure. I know that," I said, not knowing it at all.

"Well then?" The officer yawned, not caring how loudly he declared his boredom over my future career. "What kind of academic experience *do* you have?"

"Well, I once made a gun rack in shop class," I said, proudly.

"Really?" he added, dryly. He pulled the notepad back to where it had been previously and the scribbling began again.

"Oh, yeah!" I said. "And my Grampa *really* loved it!"

"Uh, yeah. Whatever. I don't care." He stood, grabbed a bunch of papers, stamped them, and shoved them into my chest. "Here," he said. "Take these over to that lady there. The one with the big feet."

Perhaps it was the anxiety of the moment that sobered me up. I had no idea, but I now saw the woman for exactly what she was: a colossal mass of a maiden with eyes as wide as an owl's and a waist wider than a California Redwood.

"Hmmmm," she said chuckling, as she scrutinized the stamps on my forms. "Looks like you're going to be a *pecker checker!*"

"A *what?*" I said.

"You know," she said.

"No, I *really* don't!" Nothing that had *ever* happened in Bruce's Wash-n-Blow had prepared me for this.

"A Medical Corpsman," she said. " 'Pecker Checker' is a nickname, I guess you could say."

It was a moniker I'd known nothing about before that minute and it was too late to change my "career choice." The ink had already dried. I'd have to carry that badge of dishonor with me always. Worse was the fact that my entire company knew about it.

And that silly nickname did nothing but make group showering all the more uncomfortable.

Saluting Pigeons

I've never understood the purpose of a pigeon, other than their work to ruin pictures by sitting on statues. Also, it bothers me greatly that I've never seen a baby pigeon *anywhere*. I know they have to exist, but I don't know where they are. It's a mystery that has never satisfactorily been explained.

I imagine an elderly person, propped up on a park bench in their twilight years, tossing food to a group of pigeons, and contemplating the serenity of a life well spent. This picture helps put the charm of those birds into a nice, tranquil perspective. But that image quickly fades when I envision them flying away, depositing their excrement squarely on the shoulders of those below. I don't dislike pigeons, mind you. I just don't "get" them.

In basic training they were everywhere! Those little bobbing heads looking untrustingly at everything and dodging about like crabs. Always managing to fly away at the last second.

Or, in my case, not fast enough.

Leaving the mess hall one evening, I noticed a few of them lingering just outside the exit of the galley. As I began my return to the formation of my company, I happened to jostle a few pesky pigeons out of my way with a casual whisk of my right foot … a simple, sweeping motion. Much like a ball player would do in the batters box when wiping dirt off home plate with his cleat. To my surprise, though, I actually managed to make contact with a few.

To me it was a nonchalant brush. One or two sideways staggers and they all flew off just fine. But to my company commander, who was nearby, it was as if I was kicking his grandmother through goal posts from mid-field. As retribution, I was ordered to make amends.

"Apologize!" my company commander snapped.

"How, sir?" I asked.

"By saluting!"

"*Who?* The birds? *Really?*"

Apparently it was the wrong set of questions, with the wrong intonation.

"Yes, the birds!" he barked. "Salute them! Each and every one of them!" He brought himself inches from my face. *"Individually!* Do you hear me?" He began pointing at each bird, sounding out each letter along the way. "I-N-D-I-V-I-D-U-A-L-Y."

I noted he'd spelled the word I-N-C-O-R-R-E-C-T-L-Y, but thought better of pointing that out.

I had no case to argue. I had committed the crime, and there were witnesses. The judge had spoken, and the sentence had been rendered. "Sir, yes, sir!" I said.

"And don't come back till nightfall!" With that, he walked away with the rest of the company.

Raising your hand in school—and never getting called on—is always an exhaustive workout. A couple of minutes with your fingers outstretched toward the ceiling, one's upper limb tends to get quite sluggish. It's only natural. But after ten minutes of saluting birds in rapid succession, the arm begins to feel *absent.*

I snapped my arm back and forth and up and down for what had to have been thousands of times, gesturing respect to each and every bird that bobbled its way past my post. Hours later, as the sun finally set, I returned to the barracks. Walking back convinced my arm had been anesthetized; I shook my head in bewilderment. Not at the discipline that was handed down, but because I had realized, once again, that out of the scores of pigeons I'd seen that day, not a single one had been a baby.

And I pondered: if there were no babies, where *do* those things come from?

The Catch-Edge Fairy

Military lingo is something the Armed Forces prides itself on. Instead of kitchens and guns, they have galleys and weapons. They even have names for parts of the bedding. The stitching area on the top sheet, for instance, they call the "catch edge." And, if it's not facing the mattress when making your bunk, you weren't paying attention.

An unkempt bed in basic is akin to a declaration of war. Allowing your "catch edge" to face in the wrong direction takes you one step toward the proverbial gallows.

One morning, during a routine inspection, my bunk was singled out. From the reddening of my company commander's face and the veins in his neck on the verge of detonating, it was obvious something was wrong. After shouting a few familiar insults, he hurled at me a series of explicit suggestions. Physical acts, he said, to implement upon myself without delay. I actually stopped to think about his "F-words" and concluded those moves would be impossible. Looking at my bunk, I discovered what unleashed his "F-ing" fury. My catch edge was downside up.

As a magician pulls away a tablecloth without disturbing the plates, my sheet was yanked with one quick tug. Then, without a word, it was thrown over my head. I was ordered to stretch out my arms, traipse around the barracks, and repeat, "I am a catch-edge fairy! I am a catch-edge fairy!"

Fortunately for me, anyone who laughed was immediately subjected to the same humiliation.

Sometimes even boys-to-men in basic training cannot help themselves. Within minutes, a collection of catch-edge fairies were plodding among rows of overturned bunks, each one flipped upside down whether they'd been in tip-top-shape or not. A dozen men destined to defend our country, running through a military barracks with sheets over their heads, flitting like Casper.

So there I was, the original catch-edge fairy of my company...a pigeon saluter...a pecker checker...a toothbrush toilet-scrubber...a smart-aleck from the Midwest as far out of his element as he'd ever been...at least for a while.

And not a bikini-clad girl or a white sandy beach in sight.

CHAPTER 4

Radio Dazed

"I wrote a song, but I can't read music.
Every time I hear a new song on the radio I think, "Hey,
maybe I wrote that."

—Stephen Wright

I n the summer of '89, the military assigned me to a naval hospital in
Charleston, South Carolina. After six months of "medical school,"
I was a paramedic. This was an alarming realization for someone
who, just a year earlier in boot camp, was learning how to spit-shine
commodes with a toothbrush.

My work schedule consisted of one twenty-four-hour shift at the
hospital followed by three consecutive days off. With nothing to do for
half the week, I was afforded the chance to either get into a lot of trouble
or find something productive to occupy my spare time.

Remarkably, I chose the latter.

My full-time commitment to Uncle Sam allowed part-time opportunities in the civilian sector. I decided to attend the local university with a major in journalism, hoping, at some point, to find a job in radio or television.

One morning, after a late night "study session" at my friend's dorm, I awoke from a nightmare in a cold sweat. As I tripped over empty bottles in search of the porcelain god, I tried to piece the scattered moments of my dream together.

I was tending bar ... not much of a stretch given the fact the dormitory floor now resembled a moonshine distillery. Not so clear however, was the murky image of my mom, a nun from the parochial school, and my company commander walking into my bar, taking a seat and giving me advice.

"Obstacles!" They shouted in unison. "Get over them. The rules of the world aren't going to be changed for you."

The dream was so creepy and its effects so far-reaching, I decided I would change my study habits, and trade alcohol for a semester in classical music study.

A few hours later, after my third Alka-Seltzer cocktail, I thought about that dream again. Those rules. Those obstacles I'd have to overcome. Successfully clearing hurdles of beer bottles on the way to the bathroom in total darkness was one thing. But "rules of the world"— that seemed far more daunting. Then again, I reasoned, if my problem-solving mom could make money by taking a paintbrush to a bunch of rocks, surely I could find a way to be just as innovative.

As an enterprising freshman with dogged determination, I opened the phone book's yellow pages to the radio station section. Using a highly scientific method for choosing an employer, I closed my eyes and pointed. When I opened them, my finger had landed on WSSB 98 ROCK, Charleston's Classic Rock Station. I called the program director, offered my services for free, and was hired over the phone.

The following morning, I was sweeping floors, making coffee for the DJs, and filing records in a dank, musty-smelling room full of scratchy-sounding vinyl.

The radio station was thrown together in a converted efficiency apartment on the second floor of a dilapidated two-story beach house. The house, which stood miraculously on wobbly stilts, was owned and occupied by Irma, a crusty woman in her mid-eighties who spoke Spanglish, hated music and pretty much all things loud and happy.

Our rented studio smelled of stale beer, the equipment was held together with duct tape, paper clips, and glue, and the walls were stained with God-only-knows what. I worked the midnight-to-six shift, mostly flipping records, but was eventually able to "crack" the mic once an hour to read the local weather. I was a real DJ.

Though the songs were great and my imagined fan-base growing, my first gig was tainted by our restless landlord. Irma was too old to climb the stairs so, to strip away what little fun I was having, she resorted to pounding on the ceiling with a broomstick when things got too noisy.

"Ratchet it down!" she'd scream, adding a colossal knock of the broom.

"What?" I'd shout back down.

"The noise! Turn it down!" she'd say again, banging two or three more times before yelling at me in Spanish.

"I can't hear you, Irma. The music's too loud!"

We'd go on like that for hours.

The glamorous image of radio, like the military, was shockingly different from the reality. But my career in broadcasting was finally taking off, so I could live with whatever disappointments of truth came my way.

Within a month, I started reading a few commercials. The station had very few listeners, which meant most of its clients were small stores and mom-and-pop shops selling various and sundry. Some could only afford commercials in the middle of the night — read live from 4x6 index cards.

The scripted copy was bland and I was told not to deviate ... not by one single word.

"Read this card," my program director dictated. "*Exactly. As. It. Is. Written,*" he said, poking the card. As. He. Spoke. But, after countless days of reciting the same liner notes, I felt I could do it from memory. Besides, my journalism professor had instructed me that reading from cards just didn't sound natural on the air.

Our biggest client was Sal's Simoniz Car Wash where, for $5.00, you could feel good about having a nice, clean automobile. At half past three in the morning, it was time to read the index card describing their car wash promotion. I saddled up to the mic, ready to impress anyone listening at such an hour.

I must have been tired that night. Instead of saying what I should have, I proceeded to tell the city of Charleston—a city known for its swooning Southern belles and fine, upstanding gentlemen—how one could get *sodomized at Sal's* for less than ten bucks.

That was my last night on the air on WSSB.

But I'd gone out in a blaze of glory. Not from an old lady intent on killing me with a wooden handle, but because of a sleep deprived haze. I'd inadvertently told my listeners where they could receive certain sexual acts for a discounted price.

Practices, I'm sure, were illegal in the state.

The nice thing about radio is there are lots of stations. Make a mistake at one place, chances are pretty good you can go across the street and start over. And that's exactly what I did. Within no time, I found work at a Top 40 radio station, 95-SX.

Once again, I was hired to do more filing. But this time in a nicer building: a two-story redbrick edifice that housed a law firm on the ground floor. The station consumed the entire upstairs. All the desks were meticulously aligned and every Tuesday a cleaning crew sprayed fragrances of potpourri and gardenias. The audio board had buttons that blinked instead of big, clunky knobs that wouldn't turn. Even the music room was different. Thousands of neatly stacked CDs aligned in clear, plastic cases. Far different from the sloppy collection of aging LPs, each shoved haphazardly into the wrinkled paper sleeves I'd grown used to.

I slid back into the familiar midnight-to-six shift. There were no commercial spots running at that hour, which meant I was free to talk about whatever I wanted, as often as I wanted. I created my own show, choosing the music I preferred with the commentary of my choice. There was, however, one catch. The station's program director agreed to give me complete reign over the airwaves, provided I made occasional appearances as the station mascot, a frog.

"Sure," I said, when he told me. "No problem."

I mean, how bad could it be?

Well …

It's one thing to don the neoprene frog head while handing out bumper stickers and cassettes in front of fast-food restaurants. It was something else entirely when they hired a choreographer to teach me how to dance while doing so.

My instructor—a "Flower Child" throwback hippie named Autumn—never stopped talking about Woodstock. She wore patchwork skirts with double-layered tank tops and her hair in braided pigtails. Autumn took her granola status seriously. To protect it, she avoided baths at all costs so as not to dislodge any *Mother Earth*, as she called it, from its natural habitat. Autumn lived in a tent in the woods and I was most eager to hear how she adapted. She was a patchouli-infused Snow White, playing impromptu tambourine concerts for animals. She grew her own food, yet never considered plowing her legs with a razor. When Autumn began telling me how leaves were more environmentally safe than toilet paper, my interest began to wane.

"I want you to *feel* the dance," she'd say, slowly, while closing her eyes and rolling her head in circles.

I felt nothing. I just stared. She grabbed my hands and moved them along with hers in time to the music. "Can you *feel* it now?" she asked.

I *wanted* to feel what she felt, but I'd been told mushrooms would show up on a drug test.

After an hour of sweating in a cramped, mirrored workout room, Autumn's aroma was worse than the smell at 98 ROCK. And *I* was the one wearing the full-bodied frog suit.

The stations promotions calendar was quickly becoming my nemesis. Every day, as I showed up for work, I'd slink my way up to my inbox to see what new demoralizing forum of public ridicule was waiting for me. One day, as I resigned myself to another anticipated "A-Bomb" assignment, I was pleasantly surprised to learn I had been booked for an appearance as myself—an on-air personality. "*Hit-Man Dan, The One-Man Party*" was finally going where he belonged. The spotlight!

My audience?

Several hundred middle school kids at a "Just Say No to Drugs" event. The fact that none of the other on-air celebrities wanted to take on this assignment never even entered my mind.

I should have smelled disaster looming.

I arrived early, before the busload of students, practicing my introduction in my best radio voice. "Hey, there! How *you* doin'?" I said, delivering the line over and over to the tree next to me. Finally happy with the result and ecstatic no one saw me doing it I practiced my autograph in an artfully illegible mark of celebrity.

Never underestimate the intelligence of a kid. No matter how young they look, they're cleverer than you think.

"What's *your* name?" I shouted, rather condescendingly, at a kid sporting a ponytail, sitting under a nearby tree.

"Why do you care?" he shot back, quickly getting up and making double-time in my direction.

"Uh, I don't know. I'm just supposed to ask it." I said defensively, taken aback somewhat as he got closer. Something about this kid reminded me of ... someone. "Besides," I added, "It's just what they told me to say."

"Yeah? Well, you're on a need-to-know basis. And you *don't* need to know."

Suddenly, he didn't look so little anymore. In fact, he kind of scared me. He was a foot taller and easily had twenty pounds on me.

"Here," I said, trying to hand him a cassette as a peace offering. "Stay off drugs!"

"Why?" he asked, shoving it back at me.

"Uh, cuz they're not good. That's why."

"That's the best you've got?" he answered. "Cuz they're not good? My *mother* can do better than that ... and she knows *nothing* about staying off drugs. Trust me."

"Look ... no one told me I was supposed to *answer* questions."

"Well, answer me this: have *you* done drugs?" he asked.

"We're not talking about me," I quickly pointed out.

"So you *have*."

"I didn't say that. Listen!" I said, more than ready to end this conversation. "You want the cassette or not?" I shoved it at him; he looked it over.

"What is this? *Madonna*?" he snapped back. "Really?"

"What is it everyone has against her?" I said, looking at the tape now at my feet.

"You got any Jethro Tull?" he asked.

Seriously? That familiar feeling began to take shape. "You're not from Missouri, are you?"

He walked away shaking his head.

"Hey!" I yelled after him. "She's better than *Starship!*"

With the exception of my juvenile delinquent friend, handing out music and tee shirts while telling each kid to "Stay off drugs!" made me feel like a bona-fide rock star! With just three words and some giveaways, I was a legend to a whole age group…a legend-in-my-own-mind, of course, but a legend nonetheless.

With nothing left to give away and no more advice to dispense, I looked first at my watch—several hours had passed—and then around to see the buses now lining up to take the students home.

The return trip to Charleston had just one route—a narrow two-lane highway that went on for nearly twenty miles. Not wanting to get caught in the traffic jam of buses, I left ahead of the kids.

On the drive home, I thought of all the stories I would share with my friends and family. How I had surely made a difference. I had, no doubt, changed lives. And, after a few more radio remotes, I was confident I'd be drafting my speech to the Nobel Laureate Commission.

I could see it all so clearly. Standing at the podium, accepting my Medal of Honor as flash bulbs burst all around. While practicing my parade wave, I noticed flashing bulbs of a different kind—the "official" kind—coming up quickly behind me.

I pulled to the side of the road and endured the horrified wait of anyone pulled over by a patrolman. A look in my rearview mirror showed the officer ambling toward my window. His image grew, puffing and waddling, and with a sour expression splashed across his face. I had no idea how long he'd been behind me but, from his grimace, it was pretty clear he'd been in pursuit for quite some time.

"Do you know how fast you were going?" he asked.

"No," I quipped.

Without a word, he began writing my first ticket. Speeding. Twenty-five over the limit.

"Do you know who I am?" I asked.

"I will in a minute," he said.

I chuckled, "Well, you should know that I'm *Hit-Man Dan! The One-Man Party!*"

Clearly unimpressed with my celebrity, the officer caught sight of my next infraction. "Seat belts are not only important, son, but legally required for everyone on the road," he said.

He started working on Ticket #2.

"Hit-Man …uh …Dan? I'd like to see your license now if you don't mind."

Though not at all happy with the obvious lack of respect I was being given, I dutifully handed the license over. He held it in his beefy hand, peered down upon it, and rolled his eyes. Then, as if he'd just experienced a sudden headache, he rubbed his forehead.

Expired license. Ticket #3.

His irritability seemed to grow as he flipped the pages of his ticket book, probably looking for more space. It was clear we were going to be here for a bit.

As my detainment drew on, so too did the mountain of paperwork. "I need for you to turn on your hazards," he dictated. I sat back and resigned to the process. As he hesitated near my elbow, an exhaustive exhale told me another problem had just surfaced. A requirement of state law was yearly vehicle inspections. Proof of compliance was a sticker affixed to the lower left-hand corner of the windshield. Mine was in the proper position, but that wasn't the issue.

"You're three months overdue."

My head slumped to my chest. Ticket #4.

After walking back to his patrol car, I noticed the officer looking around his glove compartment in great haste. I figured his pen had run out of ink. When he found what he was searching for, he looked up in anger. Before I could brace for another blow, he was at the window again. "You know you have a tail light out?" His annoyance was now exasperation.

Ticket #5.

It was too much. I jumped out of the car in protest. "It's not out. Really. I can show you. It's just loose. Honest. This one is *not* my fault."

I rounded the trunk, popped the latch and lifted the lid. A wave of shock and horror swept over me. An array of crushed beer cans lay exposed along the old carpet of the dingy, red, Ford Escort.

"Just getting back from a '*One-Man Party*?" he asked.

"No, sir."

"You get all this with a fake ID?" the officer asked me, craning his neck to glare into the car.

"Well now, that would be illegal, wouldn't it?" I flashed a grin, hoping for mercy. Trying to look like the King of Cool. Meanwhile, he saw me as the mayor of Crazy Town Banana Pants.

Up against the car and now being frisked, I thought things couldn't possibly get any worse. Until, that is, I heard the rumbling of school buses coming toward us. I looked up to see a convoy of them rolling by. The throngs of fans I had just won over with my suave, mature broadcasting savoir faire, with my imploring words of "Just say no!" were now witnessing my ironic fall from grace.

I waved, as they stared back in slack-jawed disbelief.

As they drove past, I spotted the kid with the long ponytail smiling at me from the last window. "Just say *no*," he shouted. His laughter carried down the road.

My pat down stopped mid-pat.

"Do you know those kids?" the officer asked me.

"Uh … yeah … I just got done with an event where I … uh … told them to … uh … stay off drugs."

My uniformed foe must have felt pity. The punishment now taking place had far outweighed the crime. "Son," the officer said, "Throw out the beer cans. Get your car inspected. Fix your license. Wear your seat belt. Don't speed. And for the love of God, go drive in someone else's jurisdiction."

And with that, he let me go. Ticketless.

CHAPTER 5

Laundry Day and Local TV

"By the age of six, the average child will have completed the basic American education from television, the child will have learned how to pick a lock, commit a fairly elaborate bank holdup, prevent wetness all day long, get the laundry twice as white, and kill people with a variety of sophisticated armaments."

—Unknown

I got into television completely by accident. Another *fluke*, if you will. Although by this point in my life I had begun to question the validity of that word.

While working part-time as a DJ, I struck up a friendship with Leesa Lod, a local anchor on the six and eleven o'clock newscasts. Leesa began her drive home just as my show began; the familiar, coveted midnight-to-six slot.

She called just before midnight every night, always asking for the same song: C & C Music Factory's, *Gonna Make You Sweat*. Hot flaming Q-Tips in my eyes would have been far more enjoyable than playing that song, but she liked it. Despite Charleston being a small TV market, Leesa was a local celebrity, blonde, and a bit mysterious. I was nineteen and held delusions of grandeur, so I honored her ad-nauseam request. After a few months, she responded in kind, offering me a part-time job as her station's teleprompter operator.

It was unremarkable work, really: insert-perforated-edges-of-paper-script-into-said-slots-then-advance-pages-along-conveyor-belt. Scroll too quickly, though, and the anchors would lose their place. Roll the papers too slowly and they sounded like an 8-track tape that had been left in the sun too long. It was the easiest job at the station. And I was terrible at it, falling asleep in the middle of each evening newscast.

Two months into my prompter assignment came another F-word — FIRED! Amazingly it wasn't me! One of the station's camera operators was canned after a night of binge drinking while driving in the news van.

Desperate to fill the slot, Florian, the chief photographer, asked if I wanted the job. Though Florian suspected I'd never held a camera before, he gave me a shot. I quickly confirmed his suspicions, when, as he placed the thing on my shoulder, I failed to locate the on/off switch.

Despite the job paying just above the poverty line, it was full-time and came with benefits. More importantly, it meant I'd never have to play C & C Music Factory ever again. So, I turned my microphone off to become the new cameraman at the local NBC affiliate.

Television cameramen, I soon realized, are very much like paramedics. They too wait around for things to go wrong. But instead of hanging out in fire stations, cameramen wait in newsrooms. And when they get a call, they are out the door just as fast as if someone's life is on the line. Though, really it's just ego hanging in the balance. Sometimes, if they are in their vehicle listening to a scanner, chances were pretty good the cameraman will beat the police, firefighters, and ambulance to the scene.

The point I'm trying to make is this: you had to be quick. Get there as soon as possible to capture all the action as it unfolds.

My first "breaking news" story came on an idle Tuesday afternoon: A car crash just in front of our station. Throwing my Game Boy to the floor, I geared up in readying fashion. *This* was what I had trained for.

Despite the crash being outside under sunny skies, I—for whatever reason—felt I needed a camera light. That meant a twenty-pound battery belt being strapped around my waist, tethered to the ten-pound light mounted atop my camera. It took me nearly half an hour to "gear up." With a portable recording deck dangling from one shoulder, a camera balancing gingerly on the other, and a thirty-pound, metal tripod slipping from underneath my arm—I lumbered down the street—anxious to get what pictures I could. I looked like …uh… what was that word…microphallus … headed toward a 4-alarm blaze. In reality, all we had here was a tiny ember trying to spark.

You can imagine my disappointment, when I got to the scene of the crash. The accident had already been cleared.

I walked back, a little skittish, to the newsroom. Carrying with me video of only broken glass and a curb with black tread marks. Dropping pieces of expensive, heavy equipment along the way, I rehearsed innumerable excuses of how I had managed to miss, entirely, an accident in the parking lot of our very own newsroom. Worse was the feeling I had when I looked through the camera lens and saw only black and white.

"I broke the color thingy," I said to Florian, as I snuck into the newsroom from the backdoor.

"What are you talking about?"

"You know, the color thingy that you look through," I said. "I think I broke it."

"The viewfinder?"

"Is that what it's called?"

The look on Florian's face told me the *viewfinder* wasn't broken at all. Florian threw a manual at me, told me to read it, and advised me never to share the "color thingy" story with anyone in the newsroom, or I'd endure a never-ending ritual of being laughed at.

A few days later, just as I was leaving the newsroom for the evening, I overheard some chatter on the scanner about a fire in Summerville, a town north of Charleston. My reporter Dan Krosse wanted to be on every assignment. He loved the rush of a deadline and the opportunity to craft a really great story. The adrenalized look in his eyes as he listened to the Summerville report on the scanner, even at that late hour, told me I was going to have to run just to keep up with him.

Dan and I jumped into our news vehicle and took off for the location. Late night stories were the easiest to get to. There was less traffic and fewer cops, which meant speeding was presumed. Even as I sped, Dan urged me to drive faster.

We got there in record time. The fire trucks and ambulances waiting in line along the road told us we were *on scene.* But there weren't any flames. Just a red/orange glow in the distance, and that was from the light bars of the emergency vehicles. We parked our news van alongside a fence. Shimmying up the van's ladder with my camera, we stood on its roof to get a better view. The glow of the vehicles seemed to move closer, surrounding us on all sides. Remembering where the power switch was, I flipped the camera on. Just then, fire trucks started whizzing past us at breakneck speed. One by one, they seemed to be retreating. Suddenly we found ourselves in the middle of the danger zone.

Still, no flames.

Just then, a fire fighter stepped up to the front of our news van in full gear. He looked up and yelled through his oxygen mask, "What do you think you're doing here?"

"Our job," Dan shouted back.

"You're in the thick of it!" The words were barely audible through his mask. He pointed back to the roadblock Dan and I had conveniently ignored.

"I don't see any flames," Dan, in a patronizing tone, shouted back.

"There wouldn't be," he chided. "It's a *chemical* fire. It's the compounds in the air we're worried about. Not flames. The wind just shifted and you're contaminated now. Completely."

He snickered before he continued. "You're gonna need to come with us for DECON."

Realizing we were the only ones around not wearing a gas mask, we followed his orders to the letter.

We were directed to a HAZMAT location, the headquarters of the multiple units fighting the chemical fire. Everyone's masks had been removed, so I felt an air of safety. That feeling didn't last long.

"Stand over there," an authoritative voice came from the blackness.

"Where?" I said, looking around, clueless.

"Over there," he said.

Again. Nothing visible. I thought the chemicals might have seeped into my eyes. Dan finally interjected.

"Look," he said. I knew Dan well enough to know he was losing his patience. "I don't see anything. Just *what* is it you want us to do? *Where* do you want us to go?"

It was then I noticed an inflatable kiddie pool with three inches of standing water. It was tucked alongside a small clump of trees and the official, now coming into the light, motioned for us to move toward it. The pool had barely enough water to get our socks wet. Splashing and frolicking was obviously not in the plans.

A group of EMTs stood waiting for us with big brushes and fire hoses. Beside them, half a dozen large, red bags with black and yellow hazardous tape. Signs that read, "Place Clothes Inside" were affixed to each one. It all seemed kind of serious.

"We need to scrub you down," said one of the EMTs.

"Stand in the pool. We'll hit you with some Epsom Salt. Brush it in. Then wash it off. No big deal."

Sure, it wasn't a big deal to *him*. *He* was going to stay dry.

Dan went first. Stripped down to his boxers and, with his arms outstretched, he was doused with salts and powders and scrubbed down with brushes like you'd find at a do-it-yourself carwash. Watching him, I laughed. Standing there in a tiny pool of water, in the middle of the woods, and in the middle of the night. I could almost hear banjos playing in the distance.

Next, it was my turn for deliverance from chemical poisoning. I stood there, fully clothed with only my shoes and socks off. With brush in hand, an impatient EMT waited for me to strip down to my boxers. I didn't move.

"C'mon!" he said. "I haven't got all night."

Again, I just stood there.

"You do speak English, right? Clothes. Off. Now."

"Uh, I can't," I more-or-less, whispered.

"Why not?"

"It's … uh … it's … uh …" I motioned for him to come closer. "It's kind of … uh … It's *laundry* day."

"What does that mean?"

I knew I wasn't getting anywhere nor would I get anywhere with this guy, so I slowly began to undress. Placing my clothes in the red bag, timidly folding each item, stalling for as much time as I could. Hoping an exit strategy would pop into my head.

It didn't.

Suddenly, there I was—naked in a kiddie pool of water…in the middle of the woods…in the middle of the night. To make matters worse, the water was freezing. My shortcomings recessed immediately. Dan stared at me with a rapt expression, then turned away to hide the laughter.

Thinking the worst was over; I dried myself off with a towel, never happier to have been in the company of cotton. Thinking no one would ever have to know. As quickly as I convinced myself of that, I was handed a balled-up, orange, paper heap of something.

"What's *this* for?" I asked inquisitively.

"The hospital. You need something to wear," said the EMT. Pointing to the bag, he continued, "Your clothes are all contaminated."

I was fitted with an orange paper suit, a one-size-fits-all-but-me kind of thing. I instantly donned the fashion persona of a human traffic cone. The indignity apparently not ending with being the naked man in the woods.

"We're taking you to the hospital for another round of examination," the man said.

It's one thing, I suppose, to have something like this happen in the darkened woods where very few can see. It's quite another to walk into a hospital with glaring bright lights and dozens of people who are trained to put their eyes on you. So much for the notion this would all be swept under some giant rug.

Arriving at the hospital, I jumped out of the back of the ambulance and plodded through the front door. Dressed in paper prison garb, I looked like a medical fugitive. The paper suit had started to tear in all the wrong places.

I was guided to X-ray where I was placed in front of a large, metal slab.

A female attendant entered the room. "I need to get some pictures," she said, grabbing my zipper at the neck, quickly inching it downward.

"Whoa!" she added, speaking as one might talk to a horse about to run off a cliff.

Abandoning the zipper, she looked at the ceiling and put both hands up. "Laundry day?" she asked.

"Yep."

A few hours later we were cleared. No chemicals. No problems. Just a bit of humiliation.

I was so close to going home. Instead, I was now standing in a hospital parking lot, grabbing my crotch, and looking as if I'd just escaped from a chain gang.

I had to get out of this job. Had to get away from this town, in fact. It was time for me to move out. Move *up*.

I needed a bigger *viewfinder* to peer through.

CHAPTER 6

"His Airness" and The Little Man

"I've missed more than 9000 shots in my career. I've lost almost 300 games. 26 times, I've been trusted to take the game winning shot and missed. I've failed over and over and over again in my life. And that is why I succeed."

—Michael Jordan

I've always had a great work ethic; start in a small market, move to a bigger one, then onto a network. I had no fear of the mountainous climb to the top. I just wanted it yesterday.

When my friend Cathy, an anchor and reporter at the Charleston station, took a job in Charlotte, North Carolina, I saw my opportunity to jump a hundred market sizes. I'd only been in Charleston just over a year. Regardless, Cathy told her new station about me and had them set up an interview.

Then, the same thing that had happened to me before—not knowing how to turn on the camera—happened again. In South Carolina, we shot on old equipment with very few buttons. But North Carolina was a bigger market with newer stuff. Stuff I'd never seen before. Cameras with silver switches, knobs, wheels and … flux capacitors. But I BS'd my way through the entire interview.

Again.

Convincing them I knew what everything was.

Again.

Once more, I got the job. You'd think by now someone would have caught on.

While working in Charlotte, I realized every station, regardless of the city, had two types of cameramen: general assignment, which covers everything from fires and disasters, to school board meetings. And *sports*.

A sports cameraman has the best job in the newsroom, because they rarely work in a newsroom. They are a separate department, like the weather team. And there is never any *real* "breaking news" in sports. All the games are scheduled ahead of time. Everyone knows that. Even I knew it. I had a magnet with the Charlotte Hornets basketball season plastered on the front that reminded me.

It was normal for the general-assignment camera operators to shoot the weather stories. Covering weather segments meant you drew the "short straw" for the day. You were either going to be outside in the sweltering heat or pelted by hail. It was always wise to steer clear from the meteorologists.

But if your assignment was shooting for the sports department, your day just became sublime.

One Friday morning I was asked to cover the pre-game warm-ups for the Charlotte Hornets. Like a minor league player getting called up to the majors, I jumped at the chance.

It got sweeter. "The Bulls are in town," our news director told me. The Bulls—and Michael Jordan—was the biggest thing in sports. Since "His Airness" was in the Queen City, that meant *he* was the biggest story of the day. And I was on it!

I'd never covered basketball. I'd never *played* basketball. I did get one thrown at me once by a bully in gym class, but that was the closest I'd ever come to handling one.

Covering Jordan meant I was going to be out of the newsroom for the day. The only downside was keeping my lack of basketball knowledge a secret.

I drove with the sports reporter, a tall, chiseled athlete named Dirk. His shoulders were as broad as I was high. Even his name exuded intimidation. *Dirk* said he could "palm" a basketball and bragged about how hard it was to do.

"I can squeeze a tennis ball," I said, rather impressively. It was all I could think of to counter. Dirk said nothing so I continued driving in silence.

I knew where the arena was. But, with the exception of the night I saw Janet Jackson "Rhythm Nation" her way across the stage, I'd never been inside. Not that I was about to admit that. Squeezing a tennis ball was bad enough.

We arrived early in the afternoon. "Park over there," Dirk ordered, while pointing to a curb with his name stenciled in black paint. As a general assignment cameraman, I usually just parked wherever I wanted while covering a crime scene, throwing my press credential around as if it were an FBI badge. Hoping the police would be too busy to realize I'd just triple parked in a tow away zone. Now, carrying a sports reporter, I got to park in a sanctioned lot.

We walked into the arena from the back entrance. Dirk moseyed in with a confident swagger and brandishing a credential I didn't have.

"I'm with him," I said, following behind, as we made our way past the security entrance.

I wrinkled my nose. Everything smelled like a sweaty practice jersey. I decided maybe the sports guys didn't have it so good after all.

Dirk went straight to the cafeteria but not before "high-fiving" and greeting everyone in sight.

It became obvious to me that Dirk loved working the crowd.

"Grab a few shots of Jordan," he said to me. "I'll meet you at the car in an hour."

The arena wasn't anything like I remembered. The concert chairs had been replaced with shiny floorboards. And squeaky sounding shoes had taken the place of the music. I sat under the net watching Jordan make free throws, wondering if this was where Janet stood when she sang *What Have You Done For Me Lately?*

Being the most recognizable sports figure on the planet, Michael Jordan never moved without a strategically placed array of security guards. One in front. One in back. One flanking each side. But they and he (and I) were not the only ones around. I stopped counting camera crews, still photographers, and reporters at fifty, each one vying for the perfect shot, the perfect line to write.

When Jordan finished making baskets (he never seemed to miss one), he and his entourage decided to conduct a makeshift press conference outside the locker room. I'd never done this, so I just followed everybody else.

We all walked backward, getting shots of Michael in motion. It was the proverbial walking-down-the-hallway shot, but I noticed mine looked a little better than the ones I'd seen on TV. It was ... *closer.* Somehow, in the middle of all the chaos, I managed to wedge myself between Michael and the security guard in front of him. Like a sandwich, I was now crammed between the superstar (not a small guy) and his front bodyguard (*really* not a small guy). The crowd, now surging and in near pandemonium, inched its way along. I looked wildly around for a way out but there was no time and no way to move me from the inner circle. I was stuck. With my neck craning, I kept looking up, walking backward, keeping in step with the swarm of media, and trying my best not to trip. It didn't work.

I saw nothing but legs, feet, and commotion. I was flat on my back, lying on the floor. Then, out of nowhere came an enormous hand, even larger than Dirk's. With the power of a crane, Air Jordan was scooping me off the floor. He picked me up and brushed me off.

"C'mon, little man," he said, placing me to the side of the crowd, out of harm's way. "You're gonna hurt yourself."

I was astonished! I recalled how he'd only used one hand. I sat there, shaking my head in amazement as the crowd continued toward the interview location.

"Damn!" I said aloud. "The interview!"

I'd forgotten all about it. Thirty seconds earlier, I had the best seat in the house, scant inches from the world's greatest athlete. Now I was on the outside and, with so many people in front of me, I was having trouble looking in. Never mind getting the shot.

Michael started the *presser*, as it's called, and I wasn't anywhere close to being in position. I knew all the good questions are always asked first, so I had to act fast. Looking to my left, I noticed a small metal table. Thinking I could use it to gain a bit of leverage over the heads of the reporters and cameras, I moved it behind the crowd. Thrilled over my MacGyver instincts, I was unaware of the noise I was making. The table's feet scraped against the concrete floor, making a horrific screech throughout the room.

Everything stopped. The questions. The answers. Each head turning backward to see what was causing the mayhem. As Michael made eye contact with me, I felt the earth grinding to a halt along its axis.

"Little man," bellowed Michael. "You set? You ready to go?"

I wasn't really. In all the turmoil, I'd completely forgotten to tell Dirk about the impromptu presser. He was waiting for me by the car. And I had the keys. Realizing I'd be pushing my luck asking Michael to, "Hold up, while I go get my guy," I climbed aboard the table and nodded.

"Uh … yes sir! I am. I'm all set. I'm good to go."

Dirk should have known better than to leave anyway, I told myself.

With that, Michael continued, and I stood on my table, towering over everyone. Even his security detail.

When "His Airness" left the conference room, I jumped down, running outside to tell Dirk what I had. I don't know how I managed to squeeze through the door with my head as big as it was. Nearly tripping over Dirk's personalized curb, I saw my reporter leaning against the front quarter panel of our car, waiting. He looked upset. I thought it was because I'd locked him out of the news vehicle.

I was wrong.

"Wait till I tell you what I got!" I said, excitedly.

"Wait till you I tell you what *I've* got," countered Dirk, his tone most unsettling. His arms unfolded from his chest, revealing a tape case. He opened it and held up a camera tape.

"Forget something?" Dirk asked.

I looked down at my camera and quickly hit the eject button.

I didn't! I didn't!

The door swung open.

I *did!*

Dirk got in the car, shook his head, and slammed the door. Hard!

"Maybe he'll do it again." I said, trying to sound hopeful as I pounded on the rolled up window. "I think we bonded in there!"

Driving away trying to break through the tension, I looked over at Dirk. "You know, I once saw Janet Jackson here."

He closed his eyes, gritted his teeth, put his palms on his forehead, and started rubbing in slow circles. Quietly, Dirk began counting. When he got to ten, he just kept going.

CHAPTER 7

My Life and Times in the Middle East

"Let me tell you something that we Israelis have against Moses. He took us 40 years through the desert in order to bring us to the one spot in the Middle East that has no oil!"

—Golda Meir

The career path for a TV news journalist goes something like this: work a few years in a small market for little to no pay. Learn the "ropes" and try to get hired in a medium-sized market. Work there several more years, then hire an agent (you have more money now) and let *them* get you a job in a larger market—top ten—if you're lucky. Then, after a decade or so, if you're really, *really* fortunate, you get hired by a network.

There are, of course, several exceptions to this rule. For instance, you could win a beauty pageant, which would exclude you from all small and medium-sized markets entirely. Or if you're a man with a chiseled figure and an immaculate "George Jetson" snap-on hair do, you need not worry about any of those markets either. Nor do you need to worry about finding an agent. They'll find you. As long as you look good and have a great teleprompter operator, you could go all the way.

The other exception to the rule was … *me*. My career path went something like this: work in a small market for a few months, skip the medium markets altogether by convincing people in the large markets I know what I'm doing, and bug a network so often they hire me just to shut me up. And that's exactly what happened with NBC News. I bugged. They hired … and promptly sent me to the other side of the planet.

Thus began my assignment in Tel Aviv, Israel.

Reading through my new employee-hiring packet, something felt off. I was satisfied with how I'd stumbled my way up the ladder of local news, but this felt wrong. The last time I'd been to church was during the Carter administration, and soon I'd be living in the birthplace of the three monotheistic religions. Surely someone more deserving had applied for this network post … someone with a bit more *faith*. Yet, there I was … a heathen learning Hebrew.

I had never been out of the country unless, of course, you count the time I took a cruise to the Bahamas from Ft. Lauderdale. It took four hours to get there and I only spent three hours on the island. As an eleven year old, I believed that made me a world traveler. But this trip re-defined that definition. I was launched into an ancient world where bunker shelters were mandated in every new building and suicide bombers rode buses. I didn't own a car, so public transportation was a daily, frightful experience. *Everyone* looked suspicious.

Arabic and Hebrew are two commonly spoken languages in Israel. Learning both was an exhaustive process. There aren't any vowels in Hebrew and if you're not spitting or coughing up phlegm when pronouncing every other word you're not speaking it correctly. But in no time I had a lot of *kha's* and *yach's* flying uncontrollably out of my mouth. I was excited just to get a complete sentence out but, my jaws were so fatigued afterward, I usually nodded or gave intense facial expressions as a response.

Nothing in Tel Aviv was familiar or easy. Pizza didn't come with meat and cheese. And to get bacon I had to drive into Nazareth. Every other day seemed to be another holiday, and getting work done was nearly impossible.

After a few months, I found an apartment in an international section in the northern part of the city. We were an odd group, to be sure. For one thing, we were the only people with Christmas trees within forty miles, and the only ones, it seemed, in the entire country not toting a firearm.

But, as difficult as everything was, I realized this was going to be the adventure of a lifetime. And so, like everything else I'd done, I jumped right in with both feet!

A Boy and his Camel

Life in a foreign bureau in network news was hit-or-miss. There was always the occasional eruption of massive violence, after which I'd get very little sleep for weeks on end. Then there were the months of sheer boredom, where there was absolutely nothing to do. I arrived in Tel Aviv during the latter, on the heels of Prime Minister Yitzak Rabin's assassination. The *intifada* (or uprising) was at a standstill. Both sides deciding to—perhaps for John Lennon's sake—give peace a chance. For the time being, the continuation of the Middle East Peace Process was being fought in government office buildings, as opposed to the streets.

So, with nothing to do, I did what any normal American living in the Middle East with idle time and a handful of Israeli shekels would do. I bought a camel.

On the outskirts of the Old City of Jerusalem rises the Mount of Olives. It's the most picturesque place to view the city and the best place (in Israel) to find camels. I asked around and was told that Ala' al Din, a camel driver near the bottom of the hill at the Garden of Gethsemane, had the best camels around.

Ala' al Din was well into his sixties, but he looked much older, what with his face weather-beaten and baked by years in the sun. He reminded me of an old suitcase.

I told him what I wanted.

"How much you got?" he asked.

"I've got a hundred shekels," I replied confidently.

He shook his head. "That gets a saddle," he countered.

Without being able to afford the entire animal, I went for fractional ownership. The fact I was bartering for time-share of a sloppy, spitting dromedary with a gun-toting Arab who wore a menacing black and white *khafia* around his neck, helped me grasp what—until then—I hadn't been able to admit: I so totally wasn't in Missouri anymore.

A normal camel ride cost around forty shekels an hour. Since I only had a hundred, al Din, agreed to prorate the charges. Every other weekend I'd hop on Shu-Shu, and take a joy ride around Jerusalem. It was a most uncomfortable, unpleasant experience, but I was riding high! Literally. About eight-feet off the ground. I had been given joint custody of my very own camel, and I felt like Lawrence of Arabia.

One Saturday morning, Shu-Shu and I headed to the top of the Mount of Olives to one of my favorite spots, Hotel 7 Arches. Not only did Arches have the best views of the Old City, it also had a unique dining experience; each person was given a stone block, heated to 400-degrees. Bits of raw chicken and beef sitting in a bowl with melted butter waited to be cooked by each patron. I was paying to prepare my own meal, but the experience was fun, nonetheless. The waiters constantly warned me about the rock. "Careful!" they'd say. "Hot is the stone. Better to not touch!"

They talked like Yoda. And I always touched the stone. Licking the tip of my finger beforehand, just to hear the "zzzzzit."

There were several problems with my "part-time relationship" with Shu-Shu. The first was the dismount. The only thing harder than getting *on* a camel is getting *off*. No matter how much practice one has, the dismount is never a Mary Lou Retton performance. Each weekend, as we made our Saturday swagger up to the Arches, I'd command Shu-Shu to kneel. There, I'd tumble over his hump, and roll off as elegantly as possible.

The next issue was what one does with a camel while one burns one's finger on hot rocks. I couldn't park him next to the automobiles in the parking lot, so I secured my smelly camel as best I could by mooring him to the nearest olive tree. I was a cowboy tying his horse to a hitching post outside a saloon. Kneading my kidneys with balled up fists, I'd slowly limp my way into the restaurant and leave my camel behind.

I recognized, soon enough, that camels aren't dogs. You can't cuddle with them, they have attitudes, they spit *at* you instead of licking *on* you, and they can be a bit persnickety. The first time Shu-Shu turned and bit me, I knew it was over.

Thus the romance of personal camel ownership ended.

A Canadian in the Gaza Strip

The Israeli army had located a known terrorist cell operating on an unremarkable corner in downtown Gaza City. A squadron of Israeli F-15's were scrambled and ordered to destroy the target. The next morning we were sent in to assess the damage.

What we found were demolished buildings with tangled concrete piled twenty feet high. Christine Jansing, our correspondent, wanted to do an on-camera stand up.

She pointed upward from where we stood. "There's the spot."

"You're kidding me?" I asked, looking from the wreckage to her and back to the wreckage.

"Nope. That's it. Right up there."

Paul Gramaglia, my audio operator, and I obliged. Crawling atop the rubble, looking for a vantage point, we noticed the onlookers below growing more suspicious of our presence.

Spray painted on the crumbled walls was: "Kill All Jews." And, because the planes were American made, "Death to USA." American and Israeli flags were being burned in the streets. We tried our best to safely capture what we could on video.

My family is Lebanese; I get a five o'clock shadow at noon. So, I can pretty much look the part. Paul is Italian, so his comes in an hour earlier than mine.

But we'd shaved in the car ride over, which meant the two of us looked as though we had just stepped onto the 18th green at a *Members Only* golf club in New Haven, Connecticut. We were as white as a pair of bleached socks.

Below the rubble, the enraged crowd moved closer to our position. A small Arab boy dressed in makeshift suicide bomber apparel tugged at Paul's shirttail.

"You from U.S.A?" The kid asked with a cock of his head, apparently confident he knew the answer.

I looked at Paul, waiting to see how he'd get us out of this one.

"No. Not even close," he said quickly. Pushing the kid aside, Paul leaned closer to me. "Listen," he said. "I've got an idea."

From the look on his face, I could tell the wheels in his head were not only spinning, they were gaining traction. Purely as a joke, his wife Elaine—a Canadian—had stashed a bulk supply of Canadian Maple Leaf stickers in Paul's suitcase. He had a bunch of them in his backpack. "No one hates Canada," Paul said, with a grin.

It actually made sense. So, for the next ten minutes, Paul and I slapped Maple Leaf stickers everywhere we could. We put them on our cases, stuck them onto our backpacks, and plastered them all over the camera.

The flag burning continued, but the Maple Leaf stickers seemed to repel the angry mob. Chanting epithets and burning the American and Israeli heads-of-states in effigy, the crowd marched right past us.

Tea with a Terrorist

One of the advantages of being an American in an Israeli news bureau is that you're the one who gets to go where the action is. The disadvantage is that you're the one who gets to go where the action is.

The NBC Israeli staff in the Tel Aviv and Jerusalem offices were prohibited from entering the West Bank or the Gaza Strip. Which meant that I was left to be "cannon fodder."

"Fixers," as we called them, were paid locals who could go wherever they wanted. They'd meet us on the other side of checkpoints and cart us from one location to another, setting up interviews with those they were "connected" with. Our usual fixer was a Palestinian named Wadee.

One evening, while traveling in the West Bank town of Ramallah, Wadee claimed to have scored us an "exclusive" interview. He had been instructed (by exactly whom, we never asked) to drive us around in circles throughout the city so as to confuse our sense of direction. It was a silly exercise, really. Every structure looked exactly the same as the next anyway.

After riding the merry-go-round, Wadee parked the car along a curb and motioned for us to get out. He pointed to a door, telling us we'd arrived. Grabbing my camera, lighting kit, and tripod, we walked up to the front door of the characterless building and apprehensively knocked on the heavy door. A small, metal slit at face-level clanked open, revealing a pair of untrusting eyes staring back at us. Barking in Arabic, the man clearly wasn't happy to have visitors.

He yelled louder. Wadee interrupted, shouting back from the front seat of his car as he rolled down the window on the passenger side. Slamming the metal slider closed, I heard bolts being unfastened and locks clinking unhinged. He opened the door for us and, brandishing an AK 47, waved us in. Then, directing us to an adjacent room with his eyes, he pointed his Kalishnakov toward a set of narrow stairs. We climbed them, quite cautiously, and entered through an open doorway at the top. The room was small. Its walls stained. Aromas of freshly brewed strong coffee, tea, and exotic spices filled the space. A tiny man sat waiting in a big chair under a painting of Yaser Arafat.

This was our rare and exclusive prize.

The man's name was Marwan Barghouti. And that's all I knew of him. We introduced ourselves over tea. After which, we readied for the interview, positioning Marwan in front of an open window with Israeli tanks perched atop a cliff in the background. The armored vehicles, not more than 400 yards away, swept their gun turrets left, then right, and back again. I felt the scene added a dash of drama and intrigue. Night had fallen, but the lights behind Marwan from the Israeli Defense Force (IDF) checkpoints made a nice backdrop for our interview.

For a small man, his voice boomed … through the open window then crashed onto the streets below. Marwan boasted of being a political figure wanted by the Israeli government. He bragged of how he had managed to evade several assassination attempts and took responsibility as the leader of several *intifadas*.

At this point, I began to realize what I had done. And whom I had done it to. With a good pair of binoculars, the back of his head made for an easy target. And with my lights illuminating his silhouette to anyone outside the building, I had inadvertently made one of the most wanted men in the West Bank an easy bull's-eye. The definition of collateral damage flashed through my mind.

Marwan may not have cared about the tanks sitting over his shoulder but, for my sake, I did. As he continued his tirade, taking credit for founding grass roots organizations that siphoned support to Islamist groups, Bruce Moitoza, our audio operator, and I began inching farther away from the window.

The Israeli government claimed Barghouti had personally directed several attacks and suicide bombings against civilians. He'd been on the run for months and they couldn't find him. But, somehow, after being driven in circles, we did. And that didn't make me feel any more comfortable. With the possibility of Marwan being well within the crosshairs of an IDF sniper, I imagined the conversation going somewhat like this:

IDF: (Insert radio static for greater effect) "Sir, we have him!"

HQ: "Where?"

IDF: "He's in a room, lit up like a Menorah on the eighth day of Chanukah. He's with a group of American journalists. We have him in our sights, sir! Permission to fire?"

HQ: "Negative. Abort. Abort. Too much paperwork. Damn media! We'll find him again later."

I shook my head and returned to reality.

The interview lasted all of ten minutes. The conversation ended when Marwan finished his tea. Mine sat cold on the counter to my left, still full to the brim. I was far too terrified to touch it. I breathed a sigh of relief as he left the room with armed men in tow. As the door closed, I turned off my lights and collapsed in a chair in the corner. Glancing over the window's ledge at the direction of the turrets on the hill just to make sure no shells were being propelled in my direction.

Wadee bounded in with a look of satisfaction. "More tea, anyone?" he asked, with a cheerful expression. I gave him a look that could have only registered as sheer amazement. What was a normal occurrence for him was almost a clothes-changing experience for me.

Christmas in the Holy Land

For the first time in my life I was away from home during Christmas. But if one had to be away for the holidays, the Holy Land wasn't too bad a place to be.

Christmas was the busiest time of the year for Bethlehem. But this particular Christmas came in the middle of high tensions in the region. Years earlier, a Palestinian uprising had turned Bethlehem into a virtual war zone, decimating the town's economy, and plunging the Holy City into Israeli control.

Manger Square was essentially a ghost town. What was once a place where people gathered together in cafes was now a bullet-scarred neighborhood. And all life seemed to have been choked out of the neighboring businesses.

Normally, thousands of pilgrims would make their way to Manger Square for Midnight Mass. This year, however, it looked to be a bust. Regardless, I was determined to get there early and find a good seat inside the Church of the Nativity.

I wandered into a small cafe adjacent to what was once a bustling Arabic piazza. In my abhorrent Arabic, I ordered a cup of coffee. Beside me were two old men playing Backgammon, discussing God the way we discuss the weather. Manger Square was vacant, with the exception of a half-dozen peddlers standing in the midst of hundreds of "Holy Hardware" trinkets in a wide, open square with no people. I drank my coffee in the solitude of the noiseless marketplace.

An hour later, the Backgammon game had ended, the dice packed deep in the men's pockets, and each was going home in separate directions. The last vendor placed the un-purchased olive wood crosses into a cardboard box that looked as worn as his face.

The bottom looked as though it would drop out on him and the box at any second.

I felt sadness and anger. Sad that these people would go home broke and angry that everyone had decided to no longer live side-by-side but, rather, back-to-back.

I finished my coffee and gave a generous tip, realizing it would probably be the only money they'd see this Christmas Day.

The adventure of a lifetime was taking its toll. I was mentally and emotionally exhausted. "Isn't this supposed to be the birthplace of enlightenment and peace?" I kept asking myself. The answer never came in so many words, but what I was experiencing felt more like living on a fault line. The constant rumbling was shaking everything lose. Including something inside me.

Two new F-Words were surfacing; fear and fatigue. I wanted to leave all that conflict and chaos behind. I thought a change of location —and assignment—would do it.

CHAPTER 8

"Is This Supposed To Happen?"

Three retirees, each with hearing loss, were taking a walk
one fine, March day.

"Windy, ain't it?" said the first man.

"No," the second man replied, "It's a Thursday."

The third man chimed in: "So am I. Let's have a Coke."

—**A Joke**

I got a gig at the biggest, most recognizable entertainment brand on
the planet: Walt Disney World.

I was a network cameraman, so complex audio situations was
something I never handled alone. A friend of mine, John, a technician
who worked for Disney in the Broadcast Operations Department, had
given his bosses a glowing recommendation of my *audio* skills. Okay, so
perhaps I had exaggerated my technical prowess ever-so-slightly to John.
I was confident I could figure it out.

Hadn't I always?

I was hired to work as John's assistant, 2nd audio operator for a TV live shot with a music personality. This was my introduction to the world of freelance and should have been the easiest thing for a "first-timer" to tackle. I'd done hundreds of live shots all over the world. But leave it to the production gods to create an irony of mishaps at the happiest place on earth.

All that was required of me was to put a microphone on the talent, place an earpiece into its appropriate spot, and make sure the audio levels didn't, as John said, "go into the red." I knew that color. I learned it in kindergarten.

Chip Davis, our talent for this particular live shot, was the founder of Mannheim Steamroller, a musical group that had sold over 28 million records. It took me all of 28 *seconds* to nearly destroy a career that had been going on since before I was born.

Not on purpose, of course.

The name "Mannheim Steamroller" apparently came from an 18th-century German musical technique called Mannheim Rocket or Roller. It was an ascending arpeggio made famous by the Mannheim School of Composition. I knew nothing of composition, even less about the 18th century, and zero about this guy or his funny-named group. And all I knew of Germany was that the country was pretty crowded in the month of October.

A gaggle of folks fawned over Chip's every move. Inside our small 12x12 pop-up tent, there were nearly a dozen credentialed Disney workers and Steamroller staff. Having all those people in one tiny area made me nervous. John picked up my signals and assured Todd, the Disney Manager (and, coincidentally, the one I was trying so desperately to impress), that he and I had everything under control. Todd announced it was no longer necessary for him or the gaggle to remain on set. And with that, the entourage left us to do our work.

Much the way Commanders nod to their troops signaling a move forward, John gave the clue it was time for me to do my thing. He had already dressed the microphone, so the earpiece was all that was left for me to do.

The earpiece is essential to the live shot. It enables the person being interviewed to hear what's happening live on the air—the questions, the comments, anything audible.

My stomach felt the slight flutter of butterflies. Even my nerve-wracking experiences in the Gaza Strip hadn't prepared me for this. It was as if I was back in Little League, standing in the on-deck circle, bottom of the ninth, one out, bases loaded, down by a run. Hoping against all hope the guy at the plate would manage a hit, win the game, and I could escape the pressure of having it all fall on my shoulders.

So, with just the three of us in the tent, I approached Chip with shaky nerves and an alcohol-swabbed earpiece in hand. Vigilantly, I wrapped the device around the top of his ear, stuck the little plastic protuberance snuggly into the earpiece, and proceeded to fit the whole thing into Chip's ear. Whistling while I worked. Trying to calm my nerves.

As I walked back, satisfactorily I might add, to John's audio contraption, the flashing lights, knobs, switches, and tiny buttons, suddenly looked like the control panel of a space shuttle. It was clear this was going to be a long day. But, so long as everything worked and John was there, all would be fine.

Then, just as I stepped over the tangled mess of audio cords that stuck out of the mixer, Chip asked a question I'll never forget. "Is this supposed to happen?"

A concoction of emotions ran across Chip's face: dread and concern, with a little astonishment thrown in. And it was quite understandable. Chip Davis, a man who relies upon his hearing for a living, had removed the earpiece a little too quickly. Holding it up, as if raising a glass to toast a special occasion, I noticed something was missing. It was the other half of the earpiece. I strolled over calmly; as if I'd seen it all before, and realized the missing plastic part was still in his ear. Jammed far deep into his ear canal. It was really in there.

I'd played doctor before and that was always fun. But this was a whole new area of medicine I was unfamiliar with. Staring into the cavernous ear canal of a major recording artist and seeing a piece of plastic stuck way down deep inside was *not* what I had remembered from my doctor-playing days.

The butterflies swarmed.

My first attempt at reaching it was unsuccessful, my fingers far too "nubby" to wrap themselves around the obtrusion. In fact, I believe I managed to shove that plastic piece another three feet farther into the canal.

Scratching my head and retreating somewhat, I shot Chip my best, "I've got it all under control" smile and wink, while frantically thinking of how to get this thing removed without me pushing it into his cerebellum. Rendering Chip Davis deaf and possibly incapable of ever performing again due to brain injury was not the best way to start my new profession. "Not to worry," I added. "It's not supposed to happen, but it happens all the time."

Quickly, I looked for the nearest escape route, just in case. But the Disney Monorail wasn't exactly built for high-speed getaways. And, as I thought of all the potential rescue scenarios involving things stuck where they shouldn't be, I remembered shoving a pea up my nose when I was five—maybe six—years old. My Gran had me blow a few times into a handkerchief and out it came. A nose? Sure. You can blow. But an ear?

Well, they were connected somewhere in there, weren't they? How different could the procedure be?

With Todd soon returning and Chip just moments away from catching onto the obvious, I watched my window closing fast. It was as if I'd just caught a whiff of smoke inside a fireworks factory.

I waltzed over to that place where all good audio operators keep necessary tools, grabbed a set of needle-nose pliers, and walked back to Mr. Steamroller like a self-reliant doctor determined to wrap up the operation and still make tee time.

"This won't hurt a bit, Mr. Davis," I said, with a reassuring voice.

I wasn't sure if I sounded more like a superhero or Barney Fife.

Performing ear canal spelunking on a celebrity in the middle of Main Street USA really should be on my resume. It's amazing what one can do with a good pair of needle-nose pliers. I am, by no means, a handyman. But that tool—built for fine work in tight, hard-to-reach enclosures—is nothing short of a modern miracle of invention. With Chip tilting his head sideways, pointing the area of concern skyward, I needed just one steady unshakable reach.

I was always pretty good at the board game "Operation." With precise hand-eye coordination, I could pull the funny bone from the "patient" without touching the metal rim and activating the red-lighted bulb nose. Holding on to both my breath and my memory of Saturday mornings hunched over a game table, I inserted the pliers. Out came the offending fragment. So graceful was my performance upon my very own operating table, Milton Bradley himself (had he been present) would have stood and applauded my actions.

I had finally gotten a hit, a big one. In the bottom of the ninth a run was scored. We won the game.

But then something strange happened. The butterflies came back. This time like a horde of locusts.

At the exact moment of extraction, my Disney supervisor returned. I had beaten the buzzer but not by enough. Standing there with a pair of pliers gripping a mangled earpiece just above Disney's high-profiled VIP guest, I locked eyes with Todd.

Cue awkward moment of silence.

Once more, I saw dread, concern, and a bit of astonishment. But the questions forming in Todd's mind were going to have to wait. We were live in less than a minute.

Years later, I learned that Chip had undergone some kind of medical procedure which, for a time, prevented him from performing and even touring with the band. Even though I worked with him three or four times after that magical display of dexterity, I never had the nerve to ask him if there was any relationship between his procedure and an odd ear injury.

Having learned all my lessons the hard way, when I saw him on those few occasions, I made sure I always stayed behind the camera (I had returned to what I knew how to do), letting the real audio operators do their job. And never again did I go anywhere near his ear. Lest he suffer some sort of flashback, connect the dots, and figure out that "this" was not supposed to happen, nor did it happen all the time. In fact, it *never* happens.

Well, okay. Once.

CHAPTER 9

Golfing With an Arnold Palmer

"It took me seventeen years to get three thousand hits in baseball. I did it in one afternoon on the golf course."

—Hank Aaron

When golfing legend Arnold Palmer turned 70, he wrote a book about it. I didn't read it, but Matt Lauer did. Apparently, he liked it so much he decided to come to Florida to do a story.

By this time, I was a permanent freelancer for NBC. No longer staff, I was considered a "Permalancer." I could turn down anything I wanted but, since I was getting the best assignments, I rarely did.

When New York called, they said, "We've got a nice, easy human interest piece for you." Maybe, I thought. Though I was pretty sure the story was an excuse for Matt to play golf. Not that it mattered. I was going to shoot a story *and* a round of golf...with Arnold Palmer...*and* Matt Lauer.

We set up "Arnie's" (a nickname his wife Winnie allowed me to call him) interview inside the clubhouse at Bay Hill, a golfing community outside Orlando. I couldn't help but string out names together like clothes on a line.

"Winnie, Arnie, and Danny."

I forgot Matt Lauer was even there at all. "Mattie" just didn't seem to fit.

Tiger Woods was dominating the sport around this time and a new generation of younger golfers made headlines. I wasn't much of a golf fan, but I pretended to be. What I knew were a few of the names; Tiger, of course. Arnold. Jack Nicklaus. Phil Mickelson. Payne Stewart. I am forever grateful to Matt Lauer for mentioning, during the pre-interview, that there was an Arnold/Jack rivalry. With my brain and mouth in constant disconnect, a great tragedy could have occurred right there in Bay Hill.

How strange that I always seemed to be where I know so little about whatever it is I'm supposed to know *something* about.

As we set up our lights, Arnie made sure we were all taken care of. Water, sandwiches, snacks. You name it. Whatever we needed, it was there for us. He was a gracious host and seemed genuinely interested in everything about me. Where I was from, how I liked being a cameraman, if I enjoyed golf. After a couple of minutes of talking, I felt as if I were the one being interviewed.

Matt Lauer is the same way. He's a spot-on professional, a really nice guy, and is one of the best interviewers I've ever worked with. He has this uncanny knack for putting you at ease. And when he talks to you, you feel as if you're the most important person in the room—the *only* person in the room. He's the kind of guy you'd confess everything to. I wanted to tell him about a pack of gum I once swiped from a store as a teenager, just so I could get it off my chest. If I'd already taken the M&Ms from Air Force One, I'm sure the confession would have come spilling out. Talking to Matt is like talking to a priest, except he doesn't dole out prayers for redemption. He just nods approvingly, telling you everything will be okay. And you believe it. Bill Clinton has the same quality.

But I never got to play golf with him.

Matt and Arnie talked for over an hour. Even from where I stood behind the camera, the conversation was fascinating. They chatted about growing up, their idols, Palmer's impact on the game, winning and losing. And not just in golf. Their dialogue was intimate, insightful, and I knew, when the piece made air, the viewing public would get to see only a fraction of what I heard first-hand. There's only so much story one can cram into a three-minute spot on The Today Show.

"Too bad," I thought, knowing full well we had enough stuff in the can to fill a documentary.

When the interview ended, we turned off the lights and headed out to the golf course. I, of course, had my camera so as to get some shots of the two of them playing golf for the story.

Starting on the back nine, Arnie teed up and began what can only be described as a crazy, corkscrew backswing. His follow through wasn't any better, contorting all over the place like taffy winding its way around a puller. Not knowing this was one of the things that made him so famous, my face buckled as I watched—what I thought—the years had done to such a legend.

I looked up to see Palmer's ball resting 275 yards away, smack dab in the middle of the fairway. Crazy swing or not, this guy still had game! Matt, an amazing golfer himself, ended up a bit shorter, and in the second cut.

Six holes in, we had plenty of material. Nice drives, fun chitchat, great chip shots, and long putts that sank right into the middle of the cup. Being ever the gentlemen, Arnie looked at me, smiled, and told me to, "Tee one up!"

Surprised, I fumbled for a club, almost as if I knew what I was looking for. All eyes were on me as I poked my tee into the grass. I carefully placed the ball on top, praying it didn't fall off. I lined up the Nike "swoosh" in a straight line. As if *that* would make a difference. The voice of Tiger Woods telling me how nervous he was when he first played at St. Andrews flittered through my mind.

"The fairways were as long as they were wide," he said. "And everyone was watching. All I wanted to do was *not miss.*"

I had only three or four people staring at me, but I could see Tiger's point. I addressed the ball and stared it down, confident in my ability to hit it.

"Just. Make. Contact," I told myself.

I took a deep breath, drew my clubface back. Attempting Arnie's corkscrew swing, I made contact! A loud *smack* sent my ball up and straight into the sky. I gazed in awe, beaming with pride as I watched its trajectory.

Then it began to curve.

Like a boomerang. At one point I thought the thing might actually come back around and beg me to take another crack at it. But it didn't. It continued to turn, turn, turn.

I stood waiting for the earth to open and swallow me as the ball splashed into a body of water. Which wouldn't have been so bad had it traveled, oh let's say, 300 yards. But the fact it had only journeyed 30 remains one of my greatest disappointments to this day. I could have *thrown* the ball farther than I hit it.

"I didn't even know we *had* water back there," said Arnold, laughing.

Shrugging it off as no big deal, I put the club back into the bag. One more second of holding it and I would have been tempted to wrap the shaft around the nearest tree.

Cameramen should never become the story.

We marched up the 18th green toward the clubhouse where our round had begun. Sinking an uphill, 7-foot putt with a slight break, Arnie hitched up his pants and, with a slight pumping of the fist, confidently retrieved his ball. He beat Matt in a friendly game by two strokes but, from the smile on his face, you'd have thought he'd just won another major.

The two shook hands and walked off the green, patting each other on their backs as I let them move out of my camera frame. I had the ending to our story, which meant I was now free to play. I three-putted from ten feet away. No break. But no one saw.

The catering staff had supplied us with plenty of drinks throughout our round. I placed the flagstick back in the hole and went to look for my glass. I found it sitting in the cup holder of my golf cart. That's when I realized I'd been knocking back lemonade and iced tea—known as an *Arnold Palmer*—for over an hour. Turns out I had been drinking the drink while playing golf with the guy. I tipped it back and finished it off.

I'd never get over the "finding water with my golf ball in front of Arnie moment," but all in all the day had been a hole-in-one.

CHAPTER 10

Brother, Can You Spare My Dime?

"Where are my fries?"
—A homeless man's response after opening
a bag of food I bought for him from McDonalds.

Around Thanksgiving 1999, just over a dozen Cuban refugees struggled to reach Florida in a doomed, makeshift boat. Only two adults and six-year-old Elian Gonzales, whose mother perished during the journey, reached the shores of the U.S., pulled from the ocean by two fishermen who handed the boy over to the Coast Guard.

The INS temporarily released the boy into the custody of his paternal great-uncle, Lazaro Gonzales. Meanwhile, Elian's father, Juan Miguel, was phoning from Cuba, telling the family what everyone already knew: Elian's mother had fled the communist country with their son without his permission.

85

While the future of the little boy rested in the hands of two sparring governments, Lazaro, now fully backed by the local Cuban community in Miami, had taken a firm stance: Elian would remain in the United States with him and his family.

Thus began a five-month saga in the life of a little boy, thrust into a media spotlight that cared about everything except which country, which culture, and which set of family members would shape Elian's future.

TV news crews circled Lazaro's modest home, packing every square inch of space in front of his house, like vultures descending on prey.

I was one of them.

What was once a small, sleepy street in the middle of Miami became a three-ring circus. And it grew more bizarre by the minute. Reporters from Seattle to New Zealand took up positions in the yards across from the Gonzales' home. Snow cone machines, balloon makers, and tee shirt vendors lined up alongside the rows of portable potties the city installed for the media.

The eyes of the world now focused on the tiny house where Elian was holed up. The lawns we were standing on had changed from your basic Miami neighborhood to prime real estate. The neighbors, now sensing a moneymaking opportunity, decided to charge for the space. Front yards fast became front-row seats to the highest bidder.

Like a drug deal going down in broad daylight, cash was handed over to the owner whose spot of dirt or patch of land we happened to be standing upon. Talk about a "yard sale." What we had there was a going rate for volume. A pop-up tent in a front yard cost less than a news vehicle parked on their grass. But a satellite truck sitting in a driveway meant the homeowner could, quite possibly, retire by year's end.

Movie stars and entertainers along with political activists turned the street into their stage. And like Ling-Ling and Hsing-Hsing at the

National Zoo in Washington D.C., the boy was paraded in Lazaro's front yard before a salivating media, desperate for a glimpse.

Lazaro and Elian played catch behind their fenced-in, self-imposed prison, and always just before the local newscasts began. It was a well-choreographed routine.

"Throw the ball, Elian!" a reporter would shout.

"Over here! Over here!" said another, waving frantically, hoping the boy would smile at their camera.

After a few tosses, Elian retreated into the house, leaving the masses to wonder when the panda would venture out of his cave again. The neighborhood had gone from zero to sixty overnight.

Adding to the spectacle was one of the fishermen, Donato Dalrymple, who had plucked Elian from the water. He had taken on TV status, having become "tight" with the family. His fifteen minutes of fame lasting fifteen weeks plus.

While the spectacle continued in the street, the White House was in the midst of a series of negotiations with the family, who steadily defied every court order thrown their way. Fidel Castro, now directly involved, was demanding Elian be returned immediately. Attorney General Janet Reno agreed.

During a pre-dawn raid of the home, law enforcement officials took the boy. Storming in with full riot gear, they snatched Elian from the hands of the fisherman. A photograph by Alan Diaz showed officers prying the boy from his arms as they stood, hiding in a closet. In the Pulitzer-winning shot, both the fisherman and Elian screamed at the armed gunman who brandished a fully automatic weapon.

Later that morning, much the same way TV stations carried OJ Simpson's car chase, live TV coverage followed Elian's every move. The little boy boarded a plane and departed U.S. soil. The moment his chartered flight left the ground, chaos erupted throughout the city. In front of the house, the street spilled over with protestors upset with the police, the government, and the media. Even I took the brunt of their anger, getting clobbered with a chair by an old man in a straw hat.

"Take *that!*" he shouted, as the chair crashed over my head.

I'd done nothing but show up. Still, somehow, I had become the enemy.

Fortunately for me, the chair was wicker, so it didn't leave a mark. I didn't want to hurt the old guy's feelings, so I pretended to be in pain, all the while wearing front porch furniture around my waist.

Five months of anger and frustration poured into the neighboring streets. By late afternoon, police took up positions against hundreds of local protestors who blocked traffic, threw rocks, burned trashcans, and tossed bottles into the streets. Police fired back with tear gas canisters.

By 10:00 p.m. nearly 300 people had been arrested. With bonfires burning on a half-dozen street corners in Little Havana, the police regrouped to quash the violence. Paul and I were sent out to gather elements of what was going on in the streets for our correspondent, Kerry Sanders.

Driving towards 28th and Flagler, we hit a roadblock. We noticed several cars just ahead, parked in the middle of the street with their hoods open. Other cars had been driven up on curbs, coming to rest at odd angles. Tires had been set ablaze in the middle of the road and people were running in every direction. We'd stumbled upon what we were looking for. And, since our van wasn't moving an inch, I decided it was time to get out.

"Right here," I hollered to Paul. "This is a good spot. I can walk faster than we can drive. I'll meet you back here in twenty." And, with that, I jumped out of the car and into the melee.

Bedlam and commotion dominated as rioters canvassed the neighborhood with baseball bats and metal rods fashioned from whatever they could break. Storefronts were barred shut. Gas station owners, who'd anticipated the riots, had boarded up their windows, and shut down their pumps. Protestors ran past me, screaming in Spanish. And, although I didn't speak the language, I was fairly confident nothing they shouted was nice.

Calamity reigned and right in the middle of it—me—the only English-speaking person within a six-block radius, holding a $30,000 camera on his shoulder, and sporting a Rolex on his wrist.

"Hey! You got change?" came a voice from behind me.

Startled by words I understood, I turned. Looking down, I noticed a homeless man with his hand stretched outward, squatting behind a large trash bin.

"Sure," I said, adjusting my camera and reaching into my pocket. I handed over whatever I had squirreled away.

"Thanks," he said, showing off a wide grin. His voice was upbeat; it didn't quite fit with the situation going on around us.

I ducked in time to miss being hit by a piece of shingle flying through the air. "Aren't you worried about all this?" I asked.

"Not my business," he said.

I moved on, capturing what I could from as many safe vantage points as possible. Thirty-minutes later, with my camera's battery flashing low, I turned toward our van.

It was nowhere in sight. I reached for my cell phone to call Paul, but my pocket was empty. I was in such a hurry to get out of the van I'd forgotten to take my phone with me. It was still sitting on the charger… next to Paul…front seat floorboard.

Rioters jumped on the rooftops of the cars next to where I stood, screaming epithets in a language I did not understand. I needed to get out of there.

Just then, as a wave of panic washed over me, a corner phone booth materialized near a boarded-up gas station. It was my mirage moment … a waterhole appearing out of nowhere in the middle of a sandy desert. I moved toward it. Cautiously. Thinking it could vanish from sight at any second.

Closing the glass doors behind me, feeling safe for the first time all night, I lifted the receiver, nestled it between my ear and shoulder, reached for some money in my pants pocket … and realized I had none. I'd given it all away to the man behind the trashcans. With no other choice, I left the safety of the phone booth and retraced my steps to where I'd last seen the homeless guy.

I found him lying on a sheet of plywood sound asleep.

"Hey!" I said, shaking him awake. "I need my money back."

Disoriented, he opened his eyes slowly. Pulling focus on what was, this time, *my* outstretched my hand.

"What did you say?" he asked.

"My money," I said. "I need it back."

"Not my business," he answered.

"Look," I stammered before he could put his head back on the board. "There's a riot going on. *No hablo Spanish.* I don't have a phone. I'm out of money. And completely out of patience. Give me a quarter and a dime and you can keep the rest."

Yawning, stretching, and creaking his neck back and forth, the homeless man reached into his pocket, sifted through the coins I'd given him.

"Fine," he said. "Here ya go. Exact change." Handing me two coins, he plopped down on the plywood, and went back to sleep. It was almost as if he'd been hypnotized by the snap of a finger.

I darted across the street in the direction of the phone booth, hugging my camera and dodging a barrage of flying coke bottles along the way. Slinking back into the booth, I closed the doors, inserted the coins, called my cell phone, and waited for Paul to pick up.

He answered on the first ring.

"Paul!" I shouted. "Where are you?"

"Oh, hey, Dan. Listen ..." he said as calmly as if he were at a Saturday picnic. "I notice you left your phone ..."

"Not now, Paul!" An egg splattered against the glass door behind me. "I need you to pick me up!"

"All right. *No problem.* Where are you?"

"In a phone booth. At a gas station. Standing by a burning tire."

"Which tire?" Paul asked.

Sarcasm. Just what I needed. "The only one with a non-Hispanic guy standing next to it with a camera wrapped in his arms. I shouldn't be too hard to spot."

Within minutes, I saw Paul flashing his headlights from around the corner. I ran toward the van and jumped in through the sliding side door.

For the next week I tied my phone to a shoelace and wrapped it around my wrist. I never wanted to beg for change again, even if it was my own.

CHAPTER 11

Spies, Lies, and Videotape

"The fake capture was an excellent way to expose us to what that situation may be like. Where else would I get to learn how I'd react to being hooded and paraded through the woods?"

—A comment from a trainee with Centurion

Weapons of Mass Injection

The first Gulf War—Desert Storm—ended quickly; an entire war, over in a matter of days. As a corpsman, I flew aboard a couple of medical missions, but never saw any real action. So for me the entire experience ended almost as soon as it began.

Fast-forward ten years to Operation Iraqi Freedom. I returned to the Middle East, but not as a soldier. This time I arrived as a journalist.

Paul and I had accepted a job with NBC News, helping them cover the war from Israel. Collectively, the networks knew this time the situation would be different. *This* war was going to be messy. Anyone wishing to cover the conflict—cameraman, correspondent, producer, or audio operator—was required to go through a specialized two-week training camp.

The camp, HEFAT (Hostile Environment First Aid Training) was operated by a company called Centurion, a group of American and British military experts hell-bent on finding the "soldier" in the common man. The encampment was located deep in the woods amongst the rugged terrain of the Shenandoah Valley—just outside Washington D.C. A boot camp in the backyard of what we believed to be CIA. In fact, some of the instructors were rumored to have worked with the CIA, while others were former operatives of London's MI-6 along with a handful of Her Majesty's Secret Service Detail.

Paul and I arrived late in the evening, in the dead of winter. With snow falling, the trainees gathered in the main cabin near a fireplace. "I can't believe we have to go through all this stuff," Paul said. "We go to Israel all the time."

"The n … n… networks are concerned," Michael, a camera operator from a small local TV station in North Carolina, replied. "It's for p … p … protection. F … f … from families and lawsuits."

Michael was twenty years old, had a terrible stutter, and had never been out of the country.

"W … w … where are you going?" he asked me.

"Tel Aviv." I replied. "You?"

"Dunno. I'm a … a … a …" He paused long enough to search for the right word. "I'm embedded." He said, happy to have finished the sentence.

"You're embedded?" I asked.

"That means you're going to Iraq," Paul added.

Michael nodded and turned a whiter shade of pale. Clearly, he was worried. And I was worried for him. He was not yet able to legally drink a beer, seemed completely un-traveled, and he lived with a horrible speech impediment. Before I could ask if his family had prepared their lawsuit in advance, Colin, a former Royal Marine Commando with Britain's Special Forces Unit, walked into the room.

"Now, then. Since we're all here …" he began, "I want to explain the purpose of this training." He sized us up. "It's our job to prepare you for dangerous work in dodgy areas." He reminded me a lot of a military general. "We will show you all the hidden dangers. Booby traps. Ballistics. Emergency navigation. Kidnapping. Personal security …" His list went on and on.

"Did he just say kidnapping?" Paul asked.

"I don't know," I replied, basically ignoring his question. I buried my head in a brochure I held in my hand. Spotting a shocking preview of the next two weeks, I turned to Paul. "You see this?"

"See what?"

I moved my finger down the list of things that awaited us: gas chambers, AK-47 assault rifle demonstrations, and classes showing film clips of TV reporters doing stupid things in war zones. Fairly soon, we'd learn how to locate a sniper's nest and how to diffuse landmines. We'd also attend seminars that promised to show the proper way to cross a military checkpoint of armed militia.

Colin introduced Nigel, a UK expert in hostage negotiation. "First things first." He clapped his hands together, rubbing them as if they were two sticks starting a fire. "If you get taken hostage … you're bloody well going to die."

In my oh-so-humble opinion, he sounded unusually cheery.

"But, hey," he continued. "Let's give ourselves a fighting chance, shall we? I'll teach you how."

Nigel handed each of us a duffle bag labeled, *Contamination Kit.* "Okay. Moving on ..."

I peered into my bag, which was stuffed full of band aids, Q-tips, a gas mask, and double-sided sticky-paper strips that stuck to your suit on one side and captured deadly chemicals with the other.

"This way you'll know what's killing you," Nigel said.

This guy was all too elated.

Rounding out the contents of the kit was a chemical suit, a roll of duct tape, some alcohol swabs, and atropine injectors with inscriptions written in Hebrew and Arabic.

"Use these carefully," Nigel said, holding up the green cylindrical injectors, each capped with a yellow top.

"We're fresh out of the adult atropine," Nigel commented, looking at Paul and me. "But, here ..." he said, handing me two small green tubes. "These are for kids, but they'll do the trick." He pushed at the top of both tubes, ejected the needles. Each popped out a full two-inches.

"You jab yourself ... just ... here!" Nigel said, pretending to inject the needle into his upper thigh. "The adult injectors need just one shot. But the kiddies ..." he leaned in toward Paul and me. "... They have a lower dosage. You two will need two." He spoke in a serious whisper.

"So I've gotta hit myself twice?" I asked with great concern.

"Right-o!" he said.

"I don't think I can do this!" I said, looking at the needle, which now seemed to have grown a full foot.

"Aw, rubbish," Nigel replied. "One quick stab in each leg. It's that easy. But *only* if you're exposed," he was quick to point out. "Otherwise ... you're dead, bloke."

"I'm sorry?" I asked, shaking my head. "What was that, again?"

"The atropine," he said. "Inject yourself when you don't need it and you could wind up in cardiac arrest."

"So how do we know if we're exposed?" Paul asked.

"Ah!" Nigel said. "Glad you asked. These little strips of paper will tell you." He reached into the duffle bag and pulled out the double-sided sticky tape. "Oh, and you'll need this, too." He grabbed a miniaturized booklet from our chemical kit, flipped through a series of multi-colored charts displaying the various types of biological and chemical weapons exposure.

Sticking it to his arm, he began again. "Put these on your suit. Head outside. If it turns brown, it's mustard gas. You get yellow and ... uh, let's see." He looked at a chart. "Oh, look here! It's anthrax! See it just there?" He pointed proudly to the chart.

"Uh, excuse me," I said. "These are written in Hebrew and Arabic." I held up the atropine injectors as proof. "I can't read this."

"Here." Colin grabbed the injectors from my hand as Nigel walked to another group of trainees. "See the green at the bottom?

"Yes," I replied.

"Good. That's the grass. The yellow at the top, that's the sun. Point the sun up. Push the sun in."

Out came the needle.

"All right," I said. "I get it."

"Good. Now, before you inject, make sure you—"

"I know, I know. Make sure I'm exposed first. Otherwise, I could die."

"Well, I was going to say use the alcohol swab. But, yes. You're spot on. You could die."

"So let me get this straight," I began. "In the event of a chemical or biological attack, I need to first, put on a suit. Then run outside. Slap a sticker on my arm. Wait for the chemicals to react. Watch it change colors. Match it to a chart. Then, *if* I'm exposed, decode the instructions on two atropine injectors written in a language I cannot decipher. Then jam each one into my leg with a two-inch needle. And if I'm wrong, I'm dead?"

Nigel shouted from across the room, "Now you've got it!"

Please. Kill Me Next

A week later, at breakfast, Paul leaned in over his cereal. "Hey!" he said, looking around the table. "Didn't they say something about kidnapping?"

"I think so," answered a reporter from Chicago.

"Well, they better hurry and take us," Paul said. "We've only got a few days left."

Ten minutes later, we boarded a bus for another class on "what-to-do-should-you find-yourself-standing-on-a-landmine." Suddenly, a tree came crashing down in front of us, forcing our driver to screech to a halt.

"That's interesting," I said to Paul.

"So is that!" he countered, pointing to a group of men in ski masks who were now darting toward us from the woods. Hurling smoke bombs, they quickly stormed the bus with AK-47's.

"Everybody off!" one of the armed gunmen yelled.

We staggered off the bus, single file. No sooner had our feet touched the snowy ground than a burlap sack was thrown over our heads. Our wrists secured behind our backs as our "attackers" spun us in circles, further disorienting us. I was thrown into a nearby vehicle, the acceleration slamming me against the seat as my assailant sped away into the unknown.

The experience was all very exciting.

Within minutes, the car stopped. I heard the doors click open and, before they closed, a cool wind blew between the thick mesh of the heavy burlap sack still secured in place. I knew this was an exercise but, still, the heavy woven fabric closed around my mouth, making it difficult to breathe.

"Get out!" a man with a British accent commanded. Not nearly jolly enough to be Nigel. Two men took me from the car, one on each side, and dragged me along as I tripped through the cold, wet snow. Half a minute later, still blind, I was happy to finally be walking on solid ground.

"Sit," barked a voice from behind me. Before I could do it myself, the voice grew arms and used them to slam me to a floor as cold as the snow.

"Hands on your head!" he shouted. "Elbows straight out!"

I complied but, after a few minutes, my arms tired and sagged forward. A knee pressed into the middle of my back and ice-cold water rushed down the center of my spine.

"Who told you that you could rest?" The voice yelled hysterically. Our noses touched and his spittle sprayed through the tiny holes of the burlap. Loud scraping ran across the floor in all directions and, through the piercing sounds of what I could only assume was metal against concrete, I heard a spattering of footsteps move throughout the room. We weren't alone and, as best as I could figure, it had been nearly an hour since my "abduction."

The excitement was gone. I was miserable.

"Okay. Take 'em off!" said a voice from the center of the room. Slowly, my "abductor" removed the sack from my head. I focused as best I could, and breathed in unobstructed air for the first time in what felt like a long time.

There were dozens of trainees at camp and every one of them sat on the floor around me. Each with their hands on their head, elbows out straight, and backs upright. A half-dozen "captors" walked between us with weapons at the ready. Together, we were housed in a big, open warehouse. I stretched my eyes heavenward, daring not to tilt my neck. The ceilings soared overhead. All around me were rafters and steel beams. The place was cold—not in temperature so much, but more in the fact that nothing—save nothing—was in the room but the captors and the captive.

"Would you like some water?" One of the "hostage-takers" asked me nicely through his ski mask.

"No, thanks." I replied, flatly. He turned from "good-cop" to "bad-cop" in an instant.

"Why? Are you too good for my water?" he shouted.

"No, sir," I said, sheepishly.

Michael, who was on the floor next to me, was on the verge of losing his breakfast.

"Give mine to this guy," I said, tilting my head in his direction.

"Oh, so you're a Good Samaritan now, huh?" he barked back at me.

Apparently, everything I did was wrong.

"It's a game," I said to myself, over and over. "It's just a game."

But it felt real enough.

"You! Up!" shouted one of the guards. Lifting Paul from the ground, he walked him out of sight. Just to our left was a large rollaway door, an opening to the outside world. Suddenly, Paul appeared in the doorway where he was thrown to his knees. I noticed him looking straight into the barrel of his "abductor's" gun. Suddenly, the rollaway door began to drop. Just as the last bit of sunlight disappeared at the bottom ... *Bang*! A gunshot echoed. A few moments later, the door went up. No Paul. The "hostage-taker" came back inside, scooped up another trainee and threw him on his knees, exactly where Paul had been just moments before. Then, the same thing happened. The door closed. The shot echoed. The process repeated over and over. One at a time, our small group got smaller.

Half an hour later, still freezing, still uncomfortable, my hands still on my head, I slouched forward then got the startling shock of more ice-cold water. Knowing full well those who'd already been "shot" were now basking in the warmth of a heated room, drinking hot tea with dry feet in warm socks, I said to my captor, "Please. Kill me next."

"Okay. You're up!" he said. I walked the same path all the others had trekked upon before me. A trail of "blood" stained the snow beneath my feet, and I came to a stop near the rollaway door. "On your knees," my captor said.

Down I dropped.

"You ready to die?" he asked.

"Yes, please. Just hurry. My feet are freezing. My shirt is wet. I'm utterly miserable."

"Look away," he commanded.

I did.

Then, the familiar loud bang!

"Okay, you're dead. Get up! Head over to the cabin. We'll go over your grades. There's also tea and some food."

"I knew it," I shouted. "I wish you'd shot me an hour ago."

I walked into the warmth of a cabin heated by a roaring fire. There, like my vision of heaven, were all my friends, each alive and well. And warm. The reunion didn't last long. Bolting through the door was Colin along with the rest of our "captors."

"Okay, everyone. Have a seat." he said, nodding in approval at each of us. "Not bad. Not bad at all. All you Yanks are dead, of course. But some of you … some of you were quite brilliant!"

"Now, then. When your captor offers you something, take it. A smoke? Smoke it. A drink? Drink it."

"What if you don't smoke?" asked a reporter from the back of the room.

"Lie," Colin said, flatly. "You need to know when to lie and when not to. You're life depends on it." The man was serious. "There's a method to the madness we just put you chaps through." He looked at each of us individually. "If you're being walked to the slaughter, lie, cheat, steal. Whatever you can do to stay alive. And never, never, break eye contact with your assailant."

"Why?" The question blurted from my mouth before I had a chance to raise my hand.

"Because you become a human being, not just another hostage. Let him see your eyes. Maybe they'll spare you. It's unlikely. But possible."

The room grew quiet as we listened to Colin continue on with his critique of our abduction. Suddenly, each of us saw the seriousness of it all.

Later that night, in desperate need to lighten the mood, we told jokes and funny stories about our Centurion experiences. Except for Michael. He was at a table by himself. Wondering what in the world he'd gotten himself into.

And how on earth he could get out.

The Juxtaposition of the Ridiculous

A week later, Paul and I arrived in Israel to find Tel Aviv on edge. War was imminent and rumored weapons of mass destruction were nearby, just over five minutes flight time from western Iraq to the streets of the city.

With a crew of nearly forty, NBC took over the Sheraton Hotel, which sat along the shores of the Mediterranean. U.S. Patriot Missile batteries took up position in the parking lot. Our bunker was three floors below the lobby. Barricaded behind a three-foot wall of concrete and a two-thousand-pound steel door that only locked from the inside, we were assured safety from any chemical, biological, or nuclear attack. Tel Aviv was ready, even if we weren't.

Each crew had been given assignments along with a choreographed routine of what to do when the missiles began flying our way. While some of us were assigned positions in the streets (taking shelter in prearranged designated areas), Paul and I were assigned to the cameras on the roof, twenty stories up. It was a ridiculously designed plan that, for Paul and me, meant certain death.

Standing alone at the top of the building, our task was to activate the remote cameras, then run like hell to the bomb shelter below.

"You'll have to take the stairs," Larry, our producer, said. "The hotel won't have power. The backup generators won't be activated."

"How long does it take to get down?" I asked.

"About six minutes."

"Wait a second?" I asked, a bit troubled. "The SCUDS will get here in less than that!"

"Yeah. I know." Larry scratched his head, sounding somewhat disappointed. "We've been practicing this and haven't quite figured that one out yet."

I looked at Paul, then back to Larry. "Well, until we do, Paul and I feel pretty comfortable about working on the first floor."

I thought about my HEFAT training and what I was supposed to do in this situation. There were no land mines, or rampant militiamen running amok with assault rifles. This fell more in line with the film clips of TV reporters doing stupid things in war zones.

Michael, our stammering friend from North Carolina, embedded somewhere in Afghanistan, sent an email detailing what he'd been up to: staying busy avoiding the occasional rocket-propelled grenade, eating fly-infested pita bread, and taking showers with water bottles in between dust storms. He'd applied everything our training covered. Meanwhile, I had a room on the tenth floor of the Sheraton with a sunset view of the Mediterranean, a massage from a Hungarian woman named Perva every evening, and a mint on my pillow each night.

I'd seen more in my training than I did in Desert Storm and Operation Iraqi Freedom combined. I prepared for a tsunami and experienced only a wave. But I did my job. I played my role. I covered stories from the Middle East and, although they weren't the stories I thought I'd see, I was most relieved with the outcome. I didn't need to witness destruction first-hand to know it existed. It was out there, just a few hours away.

I had it easy. Others, not so much. The impact of that irony was my sincere appreciation; for the people and the stories we *did* cover, and the hardship, heartbreak, and heroics that may never be known.

CHAPTER 12

Happy Birthday, John!

"Looking fifty is great ... if you're sixty."

—Joan Rivers

n early February 2004, Haiti was embroiled in a coup d'etat. NBC had offered me an assignment covering the collapse. And, with chaos in the streets and murder in broad daylight, I promised to get back to them. Truth is, dangerous or not, I was already weighing the options of another offer from a friend of mine.

Ken had been all over the world. He was with Bob Ballard when they found the Titanic, worked at the White House, and was once taken hostage in a country he still refuses to name.

"I've got a job for you in Los Cabos, Mexico," Kenny said over a cup of coffee.

"What's the gig?" I asked, more interested than I wanted to let on. I mean, the man was offering me Los Cabos and a cup of coffee in the same sitting.

"Just a shoot at a hotel resort." He sounded cryptic. When I didn't answer right away (Haiti and tension or Los Cabos and total luxury … hmmm …) he added, "You interested?"

"Maybe," I replied. "How stable is their government?"

"Trust me," he said, putting his hand on my shoulder and looking me straight in the eye. "I think you should take this."

And with that sound and sage advice, I turned down NBC for an unknown assignment in the Baja Peninsula.

I landed in Cabo in the early afternoon and noticed the airport was rather scarce. It was small to begin with, but I could count the people inside the terminal on one hand. None of them were tourists, just Mexican Police and serious-looking officials.

"Your equipment is over here," said a Mexican customs officer holding a batch of paperwork.

"Where do I clear?" I asked.

"You're done." He shoved the crumpled-up cluster of papers into my chest.

"I'm done?" I asked, taking the papers.

"Si!" he replied. Getting through customs is never anything short of a headache. A migraine, really.

"Seriously? Because this normally takes a few hours."

"Not *today*, señor," he shot back. He pointed straight ahead. "You're car is waiting over there."

I followed the direction of his finger. Just outside the terminal, a limo driver stood tall. Or, at least, for *him* it was tall. In actuality, he stood no higher than one of Santa's helpers and appeared to be past retirement age. But he wore a nicely pressed suit, a driver's cap, and he held a placard bearing my name in bold letters. I felt pretty special, having my own driver, set and ready to take me somewhere down the road.

"A limo?" I asked the official. Darting my eyes back and forth between him and the old man, I continued, "Normally, I just take a taxi."

"Not *today*, señor," he said again. Turning to leave, he waved a hasty goodbye. "Have a nice shoot."

I shoved my gear in the trunk of the stretch and climbed into the backseat, alone. A mimosa waited for me on the bar, along with a greeting card in an envelope with my name on it. I opened it as if I were a clandestine operative—a veritable Ethan Hunt—waiting to discover the location of the next secret rendezvous.

"Welcome to Cabo!" read the card. "See you at the resort!"

It was handwritten and signed: "*One and Only.*" Clearly this was no ordinary shoot. Something was up.

"Hey!" I said, rapping on the glass partition that separated me from my driver. "What's this about?" I asked, handing him the card through the window that now inched downward.

"Sí. Sí. Yes. Okay," he said.

"What?" I asked. "No. I mean, *One and Only.* This card. What's it about?"

"Sí. Sí. Yes. Okay."

"Great," I said. I fell back into the plush seats, closed my eyes, and rolled down the window. Exhaling deeply, surrendering to the obvious: I was a hostage in a limousine somewhere in Mexico, drinking champagne and orange juice, being driven by a strange, little man who knew only two words of English and could barely see over the dashboard.

I had no idea of where I was being led and, suddenly, Haiti didn't seem so scary.

The limo pulled off the road and onto a twisty, narrow lane that careened along a manicured row of bougainvillea hedges, each one bursting with bright red and brilliant pink petals. We rounded the last bend and came to rest under a concrete canopy. My car door was opened for me; I stepped from my lap of luxury to live music blaring from every direction. Guitars, trumpets, and big, black sombreros laced with gold trim, surrounded me.

"Perfecto!" said the mariachi bandleader. "That's how we'll do it."

The band disappeared, one by one, behind a row of hibiscus.

"Guess that wasn't meant for me," I said under my breath.

"They were practicing," said a woman to my right. "*Por favor*, this way señor." Her voice was most pleasant and her smile beamed with confidence. "Your friend is waiting ... just there." She ushered me forward.

I squinted toward the sun-darkened silhouette of a man I immediately recognized as Ken. I looked back at the limo where my luggage (looking somewhat ratty compared to the locale) and equipment were being whisked onto a cart without any help from me. Then, back to the nice woman.

She beamed with pleasure again. "Oh, and welcome to the *One and Only Palmilla*!"

I unhurriedly made my way to the hillside where I'd been directed. I reached a stone-encircled campfire at the top of the cliff overlooking the Sea of Cortez where Ken grinned like the proverbial cat who ate the canary. "Welcome to Never Land." He laughed. "Take a seat. I'll fill you in."

The sun began to set. I complied with Ken's order while looking out over the sea. Whales were breaching the waters and—as fascinated as I was with *them,* I was more intrigued as to what had brought me all this way and into all this luxury.

"Okay, here's the deal ..." He reached his suntanned arm across the table separating us. He scooped up a tortilla chip from a basket I had yet to notice, took a bite, and a quick swig of his rum and coke. "We're here for a birthday party."

"Ah!" I said. We'd done this kind of thing before. High rollers with spoiled kids. "Some rich guy's kid again?"

"Not exactly." Kenny shot back. "This guy's turning fifty."

"Oh." Interesting. We'd done those kinds of parties before, too.

"Okay. Who? Another hotel exec?"

"No."

"Well, spill, Ken. Why all the double-o-seven stuff?"

"It's Travolta." Kenny said.

"As in … John? *John Travolta* from Hollywood?"

"No," Kenny retorted. "It's for *Peter* Travolta from Peoria. Yes, of course! *John Travolta!*"

I took a minute to absorb the information. I ate a chip. Took a swig from Ken's rum and coke. "Okay," I said, fully ready to hear the rest. "Go on."

"For the next few days we're going to be capturing every aspect of this party. But it's not just *any* party. The resort isn't open to the public yet, but it will be for John, his friends, and family. And it's a surprise. He knows nothing about any of this. No one does. And you can't say a word to anyone until it's all over." John's wife, Kelly Preston, had been planning and keeping the entire event secret for months.

"Ohhhhh." I said. "So *that's* why the airport was cleared out."

"Yes."

"*That's* how all my gear made it through in record time?" I asked.

"Yes, again."

"So all the planes were diverted?" I questioned. "Where are all the people? Where'd they go?"

"Never mind." Kenny shot back. "You don't want to know."

"How much did *that* cost?"

"That, you *really* don't want to know."

"Ok." I said. "So this seems easy enough, just a few friends and relatives, right? How much trouble can that be?"

"Well, quite a bit, actually. If your friends are Tony Bennett, Meg Ryan, Tom Hanks, Sean Penn, Kirstie Alley …" he continued on with a never-ending A-list celebrity directory.

Now everything was making sense. And the assignment was straightforward enough: Travolta was turning fifty. And the most powerful people in Hollywood would be on site in a relatively few, short hours to celebrate the milestone with him. Since we were working directly for the family, we were allowed unrestricted access—everywhere and anywhere we wanted to go.

Ken told me to check in and then head over to a ballroom where "some musicians" were preparing for a big event the following evening. "The family wants footage of everything possible," he said. "So grab a little of rehearsal."

About an hour later, I was in place with my camera equipment set up, watching musicians and singers prepare their instruments and voices. I grabbed a little footage, but mostly held back, waiting for more action.

A woman walked up and stood next to me. She said hello. I said hello back. She was pretty with an infectious smile. I found her vaguely familiar, but couldn't put my finger on it. We talked for a minute or two about how fun all this was and how surprised Travolta would be.

Someone from the stage hollered down, "Are you about ready?"

The woman called back, "I am."

"Oh," I said. "So, are you with the band?"

She smiled at me again. *Loved* that smile. "Yeah, I'm with the band."

I watched her take the stage and walk over to the grand piano in its center. She sat. I turned on my camera. Placed my eye behind the viewfinder and began to roll. A few chords later, I gasped. The woman at the piano was singing *You're so Vain*. Carly Simon. I'd been talking to Carly Simon. And I'd asked if she was "with the band."

About that time her melodious voice crooned, "… the wife of a close friend, wife of close friend."

I stopped recording. "Wait a minute!" I said, clearly not thinking before engaging my mouth. "Wife of a close friend? I thought it was 'wife of a postman!'"

The whole room looked at me. Carly was the only one laughing.

The following morning, I woke early enough to grab some "Dan Time." I walked out to an already-opened tiki bar, ordered a Corona, and stole a bowl of tortilla chips. From there, I strolled over to a manmade stonewall along the cliffs overlooking the water. I took a long swallow of my beer, grabbed a few tortillas, and started looking for whales.

Then things began to get weird.

"See anything yet?" said a man's voice behind me.

"Nothing," I answered, not looking anywhere but toward the glorious water and the promise of seeing the gray water-giants known for their spectacular behavior. "But I saw a couple last night."

"Well maybe we'll get lucky." The man stepped up beside me, apparently to get a better view. We were now shoulder to shoulder. He reached into my bowl of chips, helping himself to a snack. Peripherally, I could see that a woman was beside him.

"I'm Robin by the way," he said, holding out his hand.

I took his hand. Shook it. "Hey, Robin. I'm Danny. How are you?" I nodded to the pretty redhead at his side. She nodded back.

"Not bad," Robin answered. He brushed the crumbs from his hands, took one last look across the vibrant blue water and said, "Well, let me know if you see any."

"Sure thing," I answered, watching them leave.

Kenny showed up a few minutes later. "See anything interesting?"

"Well," I drawled, "I just shared a bowl of chips with Mork from Ork and Elvis Presley's daughter." This assignment, I thought to myself without even knowing how the rest of the week would play out, was going to be my landing on the moon. And once again, I marveled at how a kid like me could get to a place like this.

"Just wait," Ken said, laughing. "You haven't seen anything yet!"

An hour later Travolta's car finally came into view making its way to the concrete canopy at the front entrance. And I was there to capture the whole thing.

The "F-Word" that came to mind at this point? Fun.

The car came to a halt and John stepped out. The mariachi band began right on cue, just as they had practiced on me the day before. Travolta, thinking he was arriving for a golf tournament with a few friends, was overwhelmed as he began picking out familiar faces in the crowd who had gathered to sing "Happy Birthday!"

Showered with hugs, kisses, and well wishes, John could barely keep it together. "It has always been my wish to have everyone I love all gathered in one place like this," he said. Tears streamed down his face. It was a quite a moment.

John Travolta is an accomplished pilot and Kelly, deciding to take full advantage of that, designed an airplane-themed party. Just before nightfall, everyone was ushered into a ballroom, passing by airport sounds from loud speakers hidden in bushes. Resort staff, dressed as flight mechanics, directed us to the evening's festivities. Boarding passes passed as tickets and first-class airline seats for John, Kelly, and a few family members were bolted to the floor at the front row of the ballroom.

Tom Cruise, the *real life* Ethan Hunt, arrived with a peanut butter and chocolate airplane cake, and Barbra Streisand stood to sing, "Happy Birthday!" Realizing I was witnessing not just any ole moment, I locked my camera down, held my shot, and leaned over to watch Barbra with my own eyes instead of peering through a lens.

Scarlett Johansson cheered as a blindfolded Travolta whacked his way through an airplane-shaped piñata. Candy crashed to the floor, signaling the start of the entertainment.

Robin Gibb took the stage first, singing John's favorite song, *How Deep Is Your Love?* Carly Simon followed with *You're So Vain,* changing the words to, *You Fly Planes.* Then Jose Feliciano performed *Light My Fire.* An hour later, I found myself in the middle of a conga line with Jenna Elfman, Buzz Aldrin, and Forrest Whitaker, while the O'Jays sang *Love Rollercoaster.*

Then Kelly Preston came over. "You've been working so hard all day," she said. "Why don't you put the cameras away and enjoy the party."

"Okay." I said, not having the heart to tell her I'd been doing *just that* for the past two hours.

I made my way over to the back of the room where I shared some chocolate-covered marshmallows with Quincy Jones. We stood together, making idle chitchat at a six-foot-tall chocolate fountain that would have made Willy Wonka proud. Not an everyday kind of moment but I was glad to be living it.

Around midnight, I sauntered over to the bar and sat. "Here, have a cigar." I turned toward the voice. Sylvester Stallone passed out stogies. "They're Cuban," he added.

"Uh … thanks. But I don't smoke." *Idiot, idiot, idiot.*

"Well, you drink, right?" said the bartender, also known as Dan Akroyd.

"Sure. Why, not?" I said, as the former SNL great and Ghostbuster poured a White Russian. *For me.*

By four in the morning I was dancing with Oprah Winfrey, who was tripping the light fantastic while throwing back tequila shots. "I'm partying more than I did in my teens!" she laughed.

Just after six, John, Kelly, Oprah, Gayle King, and Quincy Jones left the dance floor and decided to get some coffee. I said goodbye to each of them like I'd known them for years.

"Do any of you know that guy?" I heard Oprah ask Gayle.

"Oh, yeah," said Quincy. "He's the man in charge of the chocolate fountain."

CHAPTER 13

"Get Me People in Spandex"

"I think the one lesson I have learned is that there is no substitute for paying attention."

—Diane Sawyer, American News Anchor, Reporter, and Journalist

An NBC intern told me, whenever she traveled with political correspondent Norah O'Donnell, her job was to carry a full-length mirror. In other words, in addition to learning how to write news stories and conduct tough interviews, the intern toted an over-sized, glass-coated reflective device for a triple-threat correspondent: tough, smart, and beauty pageant pretty. That mirror confirmed (to me, at least) that Norah knew looks have impact. It wasn't enough to just *know* her facts and communicate well; she must *look* powerful, too.

Helen of Troy may have launched a thousand ships but Norah's eyes, even though I'd only seen them on TV, launched madness and mayhem in my brain. Deep-blue piercing eyes that other camera operators told me could show through a black and white viewfinder.

In late summer 2004, the Republican National Committee organized a series of voter registration teams to canvas neighborhoods along the I-4 corridor, the area between Daytona Beach and Tampa, Florida. It was good news for the city to be in the national spotlight. Great news when I was asked to cover it. Intoxicatingly wonderful news when I was asked to work with Norah.

I arrived early to meet her before the chaos of the day began. Nervously bounding into the lobby, I anticipated the magical moment when our eyes would lock and I would know if the legend was true.

There she was, in an oversized leather chair in the hotel lobby. I spied her from the other side of the coffee stand, hunched over her laptop, fingers flying across the keyboard as she worked on a deadline. I practiced making my first impression, repeating my introduction— afraid the piercing blue power would render me stupefied, unable to recite my own name. In case the blood left my head, I needed to make sure my script was well rehearsed so it would flow on autopilot.

I walked toward her, timidly. When I'd made it to the chair, but before I could utter a word, she acknowledged my approach, "Hey," she said, flatly.

Without lifting her head.

"Hi," my voice cracked back. "I'm Dan. Your cameraman." I dipped my head a little, trying to make eye contact.

With her gaze still fixed on her computer screen, Norah rattled off a list of shots she needed for her story. "Get me people on the bus," she said. "I need shots of folks riding. Getting on. Walking off. And canvassing the neighborhood ... I need that, too." She started to raise her head. My heart thumped in my chest. Come on ... come on ... you can do it. A little higher ... a little higher ...

Just as my fantasy was about to become reality she dropped her face back to the laptop's keyboard. "Oh, and make sure you get people knocking on doors."

Look up. Look. Uuuuup. Just once. Just. Ooooooonce.

"And most importantly," she added, "get me people in spandex."

She continued working without another word. I stood there, in the cricket-chirping silence. Hoping she would glance up and acknowledge me; a glorious send-off to a man on a mission.

Nothing.

I thought of clearing my throat to remind her I hadn't left. I didn't. She kept working. The scene began to get uncomfortable.

I walked away, confident of my assignment, rolling it over in my mind.

Shots of the bus.

People getting on.

People getting off.

People riding.

Knocking on doors.

People in spandex.

People in spandex?

I stopped short of the door.

"O … *kay* …" I said to myself, pausing to watch the revolving door spin empty in front of me. "Spandex. That's odd. Is it a branding issue?" I asked out loud. "Wait … no!" I answered myself back, loudly and with a snap of my finger. "I bet she has a line about it in her story."

"But what am I supposed to do if I don't see anyone wearing spandex," I continued inquisitively. "I can go to a gym! No, no, no." I said, shaking my head. "There's no time. I'd have to contact the manager … they'll have to sign papers."

People began to stare.

I stepped into the revolving exit contemplating my next move. As the door spun, so did my thoughts. What would be, I wondered, the best way to bring up the issue. There was no easy way. I'd just have to come right out and ask the question.

I stepped back into the lobby, now completely off balance, and stumbled toward Norah's makeshift workstation.

"Hey, Norah!" I called from across the room, hoping she'd look up. I'm nothing if not persistent.

Head down, Norah kept typing. Still … no eye contact. Standing over her, I ran through the checklist, just to make sure I had them all correct.

"I'm sorry, but usually my audio operator takes care of the details. Making sure I heard you correctly … you want people on the bus, right?"

"Uh-huh."

"Getting on. Getting off."

"Uh-huh."

"And … um … people in … spandex. I'm not sure how to find those? Is there a certain color you're looking for? Name brand?"

And that's when it happened. She stopped typing. She looked up. And there were those eyes. All that blue power, focused on me. But not the way I'd been hoping.

With a look that said the dumbest man on the planet now stood before her, she glared at me. "Spandex?" she said. "*Really*? How about we look for *Hispanics*?"

There it was and, for me, a great disappointment. What I thought was going to be the look to launch a super-team turned out to be a missile that sunk my battleship.

CHAPTER 14

Steven Hawking Unplugged

"As God is my witness, I thought turkeys could fly."
—Mr. Carlson (WKRP in Cincinnati)

I've never been called the sharpest tool in the shed; some might even say I'm gullible to a fault. Once, as a seventeen-year-old in boot camp, I went marching through my barracks desperately searching for a box of fallopian tubes. My drill instructor, having sent me on the quest, did so to simply prove his intellectual superiority.

But every now and again I meet someone who simply makes me *feel* totally incompetent: dumb just for being in the same room. My cognitive challenger never has to flex a muscle.

I felt it on Air Force One sitting at a conference table with the political scientist and diplomat, Condoleeza Rice, as she discussed football, U.S. strategy, and world affairs. Somehow intertwining the three into a really excellent point and in such a way that, I thought, no one else on this planet could do. I had the same feeling while talking politics over lunch with Bill Clinton when I covered him during one of his many peacekeeping initiatives in Haiti. But I've never felt so maladroit as I did after spending a day with theoretical physicist, Stephen Hawking. For the record, I learned the word "maladroit" from the good professor while interviewing him with my correspondent, Tom Costello, for NBC News.

And for those of you who don't know, who may be at this very moment reaching for Webster's Dictionary or Roget's Thesaurus, it means bungling. Awkward. Inept.

Listing Professor Hawking's accomplishments would take up more pages than the Library of Congress has books. Hawking is an Honorary Fellow of the Royal Society of Arts, a lifetime member of the Pontifical Academy of Sciences, and was awarded the Presidential Medal of Freedom—the highest civilian award possible in the US— by President Obama in 2009. He's widely regarded as the smartest person on the planet while I was a Cub Scout who earned a merit badge for walking elderly people across the street. When I was told he was also a world-renowned expert in the field of quantum gravity and cosmology, I couldn't for the life of me figure out how makeup played a role in scientific theory. But I suppose one does need to look their best in space.

To truly explain just how remarkable he is, and how vacuous I am (look it up … Hawking asked me to), consider this:

Professor Hawking continues to contribute to scientific breakthroughs though he has been confined to a wheelchair since the early 70s due to the motor neuron disorder known as ALS or Lou Gehrig's disease. The condition, which cost him all his neuromuscular control and his voice, has done nothing to diminish the capacities of his mind.

He "speaks" through a portable communications device via a computer system that is mounted on the arm of his wheelchair. Through a computer program called "Equalizer," the professor directs a cursor that moves across the upper part of the screen. He controls it by using a muscle in his cheek. Words are then printed on the lower part of the screen and he can select any of those he chooses. When he's built up a sentence he sends it to a speech synthesizer where a robotic voice emits his chosen words.

He's also created a universally programmable infrared remote that is attached to his computer with a small, battery-operated pack built into the bottom of his chair. The device allows him to operate his household electronics: television, videos, and music collection. It functions in opening doors and operating lights.

Far more advanced than the "clap on/clap off" gizmo I use.

I mention I'm vacuous (I just love that word), or perhaps a bit fatuous (thank you, again, professor), because, while Stephen Hawking can prophetically speak on black holes and quantum physics and can create gadgets galore, I've yet to learn how to properly program my VCR. The fact I still *have* a VCR at all in my house is telling enough.

In January 2007, while celebrating his sixty-fifth birthday, Professor Hawking announced his intention to take a zero gravity flight. Floating weightless was his lifelong dream.

In April, the following year, he was granted permission from his doctors. The flight meant that, not only would he become the first quadriplegic to float weightless, it would also mark the first time in nearly forty years he would move, freely, away from the confines of his wheelchair.

Floating in zero gravity is fun. But it's not for the faint of heart. It can be overwhelming to a first-timer. It had been for me. I had to learn the hard way why these planes are nicknamed the "Vomit Comet."

Having had several flights under my belt, I was asked by NBC to help capture the momentous occasion. Tom and I were allowed to shadow Professor Hawking for the entire day, the historical significance of the flight not lost on either of us.

After gathering at Kennedy Space Center in Cape Canaveral, Florida, and using the very same runway the space shuttle has used for its landings, we boarded the plane. Accompanying Stephen Hawking for the flight was an entourage of doctors, assistants, and assistants to the assistants.

Out of his chair and away from his computer device, the professor was now flat on his back, unable to communicate. To ensure his physical stability, his cortège gathered around him on all sides. Connected to tubes and several leads to measure his heart, blood pressure and oxygen, the professor was attached to a small monitor device secured to the bulkhead just below his feet. A flashing green light and low, steady beeping from the box told us everything was, "good-to-go!" The plan was to monitor the professor every few minutes, then release the leads once the "all clear" was given by his physicians, allowing him to float freely off the deck.

Climbing to 35,000 feet somewhere over the middle of the Atlantic Ocean, we were told to ready ourselves for the first parabola. The anticipation was building. As we began the assent, the gravitational forces on my camera and me grew, which made the very act of standing difficult. The box flashed green, telling the team of doctors everything was normal. I had securely positioned myself in the corner of the bulkhead and waited, patiently, for the parabola to begin. Everything was perfect. All was going according to plan. Suddenly, I was instructed to move around to the other side of the professor to get what an assistant called, "a better shot!"

That's when things began to unravel. Literally.

As I struggled to maintain my footing climbing at a 45-degree angle and bearing two-and-a-half times my weight, I shuffled between the box and Hawking's feet. Just then an alarm followed a flashing red light.

Everyone reacted.

Was the professor in danger?

Should we abort?

Have you ever had one of those moments where everything around you has suddenly gone terribly wrong? You realize the severity of the situation and are absolutely convinced you had nothing to do with it whatsoever? Only to grasp the obvious, seconds later, that it was…every bit…your fault. This was one such moment; the moment I learned the real meaning of maladroit. And vacuous. And fatuous.

It appeared that, while inching my way around the professor, my foot inadvertently caught the umbilical of wires attached to his monitoring device. Detaching the wires had caused the lights on the box to go from a "safe" green to "troubled" red. Thus, setting off a chain reaction of horrified gasps throughout the plane. Which, in turn, panicked the doctors, freaked out the assistants, and sent *their* assistants into a near catatonic state. With everyone's attention focused on the "problem," I shook my ankle and freed the tangled mess of cables wrapped around me like kudzu climbing a trellis. While the entire team of physicians and assistants squawked and clamored over one another, scanning the professor for signs of trouble, I innocently, and cautiously, crept my way around to a new position without saying a word.

Suddenly, someone noticed the dangling leads and quickly reconnected them. The doctors caught their breath as the monitor light returned to green. A collective sigh of relief was heard throughout the plane. The medical staff was breathing again, the color in the assistants' faces was returning to normal, and I was in my new spot. No one knew a thing. I had gotten away with it.

The physicians made a final check of the professor and then nodded their approval to continue with the flight. I nestled myself onto the floor and wedged my leg into a strap to keep myself from floating to the ceiling. Seconds away from our first parabola, I focused my lens on Professor Hawking and waited for the moment to arrive. Suddenly, we locked eyes and he gave me ... a look. It wasn't a look of nervousness, fear, or uncertainty. It was a telling look. A look that pierced me to my core. A look that said, "I *know* it was you!"

Whether he did or didn't (and I'm fairly certain he did), mattered little. What was supposed to be only one trip for the professor into the realm of zero gravity, ended up being many. Apples flew through the air, as did a few ordinary folks who tried imitating Superman. Laughter had replaced that split-second moment of terror and everyone was having the time of their lives! They flipped, floated, and bounced off the walls of the airplane. To those who took walking for granted, it was just another cool experience. But for Stephen Hawking it was much more. Hawking is expressionless most of the time. But watching the smile on his face as he floated away from his chair made it clear this was truly a momentous occasion for him.

It takes the professor several minutes to spell out words on his "Equalizer" program and even longer to spit out long paragraphs through his speech synthesizer. As we debarked our airplane and walked along the space shuttle's landing strip, I decided I could more than make it to my car in the time it would take Stephen Hawking to tell anyone what I'd done. Besides, he was so excited about what he'd accomplished, I figured he'd probably forgotten all about my maladroit episode, which turned into a taciturn, vacuous event. I decided then and there, if ever asked about it, I would plead the fifth.

But, then again, here I am, (another F-Word) fatuously writing about it.

CHAPTER 15

Space Cowboys

"Is there something I can help you with? I notice you've been following me for some time."

—Walter Cronkite

I f you've ever felt overly confident—larger than life, like you're the only one who's ever accomplished anything worthwhile—try hanging out with two guys who walked on the moon. One of them being the very *first* to set foot on it. Throw in a national hero, a U.S. senator who just so happened to be the first American to orbit the earth and fly aboard the space shuttle, and that's sure to keep you grounded for some time to come.

Such was the case during my evening with Neil Armstrong, Edgar Mitchell, and John Glenn.

For nearly eight years I had the privilege and honor to work with Jay Barbree, NBC's storied space correspondent. He is the only journalist to have covered every manned space flight. Jay was selected as a finalist for NASA's *Journalist in Space* program. And, he is an accomplished author.

When he reached his fiftieth year at the network, NBC decided to throw Jay a party.

Among the invited was the NASA brass, NBC bigwigs, and those not-so-famous folks who'd played important roles behind the scenes of NASA's celebrated history. Such as engineer Tom O'Malley, who pushed the button that launched John Glenn into space and, later, took that button home as a souvenir. "I don't know how that thing found its way into my house," he told me. A Cheshire-cat-like smile spread across his face.

NBC's Lester Holt was there. Tom Brokaw and Brian Williams gave tributes. But it was the arrival of Neil Armstrong that had everyone talking.

"Don't bug Neil too much," Jay told me (Jay knows me so well!). "He doesn't do these things very often."

"Not to worry," I assured him, my mind racing with questions for the first man on the moon.

NASA has one of the largest collections of American heroes. Icons who make rock stars and actors look utterly ridiculous. These guys left Planet Earth with no guarantee of returning to their homes, their families. One wrong turn and they were truly "lost in space." AAA couldn't pick them up if they had a flat tire.

In the beginning, astronauts strapped themselves into tiny metal capsules with less computing power than we have on our iPhones. They sat atop Roman candles that shot them into space. They were test pilots and scientists, military career men and woman who defied the laws of physics and gravity time and again. Having worked with them during space shuttle launches was a luxury. Getting to hang out with them for an entire evening was enamoring.

Jay's party was held at the Kennedy Space Center Visitor's Complex in Cocoa Beach. It was an intimate affair with just over a hundred people. During the course of the evening, Ed Mitchell dazzled me with stories of walking on the moon with Alan Shepherd. John Glenn came by and talked to me about orbiting the earth. I asked him questions about being a senator and what it felt like to blast off into space aboard the space shuttle. Both men were most gracious. I was clearly out of my league.

Just as the senator turned to talk with a few of NASA's old-school entourage, I noticed a large crowd gathering in the back of the room. I made my way over to the huddled mass and discovered Jay and Neil making introductions. Like a student who knew the answer to a question and couldn't wait to get called on, I impatiently stood in line for my turn. Minutes passed like hours, then Jay introduced me.

"Hi!" I said. "I'm Dan Beckmann and I was wondering ..."

"Don't ask me about the moon," Neil said, abruptly.

"Uh, okay," I answered. I dropped my gaze to my feet after realizing all my questions were moon-related. I was at a loss. The room closed in around me. I swear I could hear the ticking of my watch.

Think fast! I chastised myself. *Do not ... I repeat, do not waste this moment.*

Jay interjected quickly. "Neil, this is my cameraman, Dan. He's the best! Great eye. Smart guy."

Neil nodded.

Jay nodded.

I nodded. With reassurance, I decided to try again. "So ..." I said, looking in the eyes of the first man on the moon. "I understand you're from Ohio?"

It was all that came to me.

"Yes."

"And wasn't Jerry Springer once the mayor of Cincinnati?"

"What?" Neil shot back. A confused look crossed his face.

Jay leaned toward my ear. "Seriously?" he whispered.

Jay escorted Neil toward the dining room, leaving me to stand alone in my—what did Jay call it—"smartness."

"I was under pressure," I muttered. Then, elevating my voice toward their backs: "It was all I had left. *Really!*"

When I got to the dining room, I found my table at the opposite end of the room from Jay and Neil. I'm sure it had nothing to do with our encounter.

For Miles and Miles

CNN's answer to Jay Barbree was journalist Miles O'Brien. Like Jay, Miles was an avid fan of anything space related. He was a young journalist, an accomplished pilot, and the camera loved him. He was also a good friend. I helped Miles shoot a documentary on the Space Shuttle program. He helped me learn to fly Cessna's. Once, he and I even got to squeeze into the Space Shuttle Atlantis together. That was quite the treat!

After the Challenger disaster, Jay knew the *Journalist in Space* program would be scrapped. Just as Astronaut Jim Lovell missed his chance to land on the moon during Apollo 13, Jay lost his chance to go into space. He and Miles had a lot in common. After years of negotiations, CNN had reached a deal with NASA that would have taken Miles to the International Space Station. The announcement was to be made the day Space Shuttle Columbia landed. But Columbia never did land and Miles never flew. Although he hadn't made it into space, Miles never tired of his passion for covering the program.

When John Glenn became a Mission Specialist aboard the Space Shuttle Discovery in 1998, I was at NASA covering the story for NBC News. Miles was there too, anchoring special coverage for CNN.

The story of Glenn's return to space had gathered the largest crowd NASA had seen in recent memory. Normally there was a scattering of people roaming around the press mound during a mission. Shuttle launches (about four a year) had become stale. Public interest waned. This launch was different. A 77-year-old senator was going into space. Not just the oldest man ever to fly, but also the first American to orbit the planet. He was a national treasure. An icon. The story was huge.

The week leading up to the launch had an almost carnival-like atmosphere. TV networks from Japan, Australia, Russia, and France sent journalists to cover the event. It was a Benetton commercial of TV people.

The day before the launch, while grabbing shots of the crowds near the countdown clock, I accidentally bumped into a guy scribbling on a note pad.

"Oh. Sorry," I said. "I didn't see you there."

"That's all right," he answered. "Don't worry about it."

"I'm Danny," I said, holding out my hand. "From NBC News."

"I'm Jimmy." He gave me a firm handshake. "Jimmy Buffett. I'm with Rolling Stone."

"People ever confuse you with the 'real' Jimmy Buffett?" I asked, laughing.

"I am the 'real' Jimmy Buffett." The man was serious.

"No. I mean, …" Just then, it hit me. Mr. Margaritaville was standing right in front of me.

Sometimes I hate the sound of my own voice.

Miles was co-anchoring with Walter Cronkite, who had covered Glenn's Mercury mission as well as project's Gemini and Apollo. The whole world watched *him* as he watched Armstrong and Aldrin land on the moon. I think Cronkite was actually more popular than the astronauts.

The day before the launch, I called Miles, asking if I could stop by and meet the famous newsman in person.

"Sure," he said. "Come on over. I'll introduce you."

I'd seen Cronkite at a restaurant once in New York, but I never approached him. A person needs boundaries. But now he was out in the open, on public display. Fair game.

Meeting Walter Cronkite was going to be the equivalent of an art student talking to Picasso. And I had a personal invitation. But when I got to the CNN set, I realized mine was not the only invite. A mob had gathered ahead of me, waiting to meet the original American Idol.

It was like the Beatles on Ed Sullivan. Except the screaming fans were now journalists. Some of which, barely spoke English. They waited in a makeshift line outside the CNN trailer for an autograph, a quick word, or a picture.

"This is crazy," I said to myself. "I didn't bother him in that restaurant, and I'm not going to bother him like this." I turned to leave, heading back to the NBC bureau. Just then, I caught sight of Cronkite walking away from the set, alone. Looking at my watch, I realized I had a few minutes before I needed to be back on *The Today Show* set. So I followed him. Closely. For a few hundred feet I trailed, like a CIA operative tailing a suspect. He walked around a corner and into a small, nondescript brick building.

"I can't believe my luck," I said under my breath. "I've got the guy all to myself." I walked in a few steps behind him, closed the door then heard a flush. Instantly, I knew where we were. And there was no way out. Cronkite stood at a urinal, and I had no choice but to take the open one next to him.

I didn't know what to do.

Speak? Stare?

I stood. And I tried to remember the list of things *not* to say in the men's room. Turns out, I didn't need to say a thing.

Cronkite turned and looked at me. "Is there something I can help you with?" he asked, a bit unnerved. "I notice you've been following me for some time."

Realizing the discomfort—for both of us—of the situation, I thought of only one thing to say. "Yeah," I said. "I'm Jimmy Buffett from Rolling Stone. I just wanted to say hi."

With that, I zipped myself up and ran out of the bathroom at breakneck speed.

I didn't even bother to wash my hands.

CHAPTER 16

Music Mayhem

"The world must be filled with unsuccessful musical careers like mine, and it's probably a good thing. We don't need a lot of bad musicians filling the air with unnecessary sounds. Some of the professionals are bad enough."

—Andy Rooney

I love music. And I hold those who have musically influenced and inspired me in high regard. But if you think I'd know how to behave when face-to-face with the artists who have entertained me for the better part of my life, you'd be wrong.

I felt embarrassment when I sat across from Roger McGuinn of *The Birds* after thinking he looked a bit too old to be an intern.

When he arrived one morning with his guitar, at the radio studio where I was working, I asked if he knew how to play. "Uh, yeah ..." he said. His face held an expression that told me he was waiting for a punch line. When the line never came, he spoke up. "Here's a song I sang with Bob and Jimmy."

"Oh," I said. "Are Bob and Jimmy friends of yours?"

He blinked, almost as if he'd just woken up from a really bad dream. "Yeah," he answered. "You know ... *Dylan* ... *Hendricks?*"

Meeting your musical heroes can be a double-edged sword.

Before an interview I did with Rod Stewart, my iPod was chock-full of his songs. *After* our meeting, I wrote a lengthy letter to iTunes, asking how to permanently delete tracks from my hard drive.

He Don't Think I'm Sexy, or:
My Day With Rod Stewart

Years ago, a TV show called *iVillage* was headquartered on the back lot of Universal Studios—one building away from my office. Since I was in their backyard, I was often hired to interview celebrities who came into the park from time to time.

The show's guests were usually D-list actors who were all-too-eager to jump in front of a camera. It wasn't uncommon to have to restart an interview in the middle of the crowded theme park because of a noisy guest shouting, "Hey! Didn't you used to be someone?"

So it came as a pleasant surprise when I was asked to spend an evening covering Rod Stewart. "The *real* Rod Stewart, right?" I asked the executive producer. "Not a look-alike?"

"No," she replied. "We actually get the real Rod for an entire evening."

Mr. Stewart was playing to a sold out crowd in downtown Orlando and we were allowed an interview. Unfettered access, we were told, for the entire night. The word "unfettered," when spoken by a celebrity's manager, usually meant you were granted no more than ten minutes with the star. If that star was a singer, depending on how well the interview went, one might be allowed to tape the first thirty seconds of their first song.

Lenny, my producer, was well aware of this trickery.

"That's not going to happen to us," he said, assuredly. "We're getting up close and personal tonight."

If only I'd known just how close we'd get, I would have turned down the assignment in favor of, well ... almost anything, really.

Paul and I arrived several hours early and spent far too much time setting up the room, which was located in the bowels of the arena. To make for a more pleasant scene, Paul dragged plants in from the parking lot and, when the security officers began their rounds, we stole fake ones from their desks because we needed more.

A second *iVillage* talent showed up unexpectedly, so Paul and I decided more things were needed to complete our Felini-esque ensemble. I dragged in a couch from a nearby dressing room, deciding to put Rod in between the iVillage anchors that would be seated at each end.

By the end of the afternoon, there were a dozen C-stands stretching toward the ceilings with lights illuminating the entire room and cables nicely taped to the floor in decorative gaffers tape, tucked behind hidden crevices so as not to be seen. A hanging plant, a throw rug, and a picture on the wall we'd stolen from a nondescript office around the corner, along with drapes we'd rescued from a trash bin in the hallway, completed the set.

Within four hours, Paul and I had turned a bland room into a TV studio *The Today Show* would have proud to use.

We were all set. Our two talent sat waiting quietly on separate ends of the couch. They'd left plenty of room in the middle for Rod. Paul and I checked the lighting. Then rechecked it again. Everything was in place. The dimmers were dimming, the picture hung in perfect position, and the drapes we'd put in place had just the right amount of fold.

"I want you to roll tape the moment Rod comes into the room," Lenny told me.

"You're going to tell him about it first, though right?" I asked.

"No," Lenny replied. "I want the reality. The *moment*."

"Oh, you'll get a moment, all right," I said. "Listen … I've done this before. I don't think it's a good idea. I mean he's coming in here for an interview. Not a paparazzi ambush."

"It'll be fine," Lenny said, with a casual wave of his hand. "Trust me."

I didn't.

"At least tell his manager, will you?" I pleaded. "Just give him a heads-up. Let him know what's waiting on the other side of the door."

Before he could respond, Rod Stewart walked in. The *iVillage* anchors stood and made their way toward the singer as Lenny coughed in my direction, then spun his finger in tight circles—the universal signal to "roll tape."

I once read that General Longstreet was so ambivalent about sending his troops into battle on the third day at Gettysburg—so convinced the attack would result in failure—that he couldn't verbally give the order for his troops to move in. All he could do was nod.

I knew exactly how Longstreet felt.

Reluctantly, I hoisted the camera onto my shoulder, pointed it at Mr. Stewart, hit record, and waited for ensuing calamity.

Paul, who was sitting on the floor with the audio bag on his lap, looked up just in time to see Rod Stewart leap above him like a runner jumping over a hurdle. He was heading in my direction. From what I could tell through the viewfinder, getting closer and angrier by the millisecond.

Rod Stewart isn't a big guy. But he is strong. Striding across the room in record time, he reached out at me. With one hand on the lens of my camera and the other on my shoulder, he gave me a shove. A gentle nudge, it was not. Like a toddler building a sand castle in the surf, then getting bowled over by a colossal wave, I tumbled over a set of chairs behind me.

Regaining my footing, I tripped over the cables, ripping up the gaffers tape and knocking over half the lights. It was a domino effect of epic proportions, one stand falling into another, littering the floor with a few broken lamps and tiny shards of glass. The lamps that didn't fall had turned themselves around, casting their light onto the walls. The hanging plant was no longer hanging and half the drapes were now flat on the ground. Only the picture on the wall was still in its proper place, but the room was so dark you couldn't see what it was.

"Let's go. I'm ready. You've got three minutes," Stewart said, coming to rest in the wrong place on the couch.

There was no time to replace the bulbs or turn the lamps around. I didn't say a word. Nor did I ask Rod to move. I just pointed my camera and rolled tape in the darkness. I couldn't even tell if he was in focus.

When the interview was over, Rod left without so much as a handshake or a thank you. The door closed behind him, yet somehow I felt it had hit me in the ass on his way out. "So …" I said, looking at Rod's manager. "About those first thirty seconds …"

Without a word, he walked out the same door.

R.E.S.P.E.C.T. — Take That Camera Off of Me

I thought getting into an altercation with a rock star was something so humiliating, that topping it would be nearly impossible.

Turns out, nothing's impossible.

There are many ways to embarrass one's self in front of musical icons. And I was well on my way to discovering all of them.

While working with Aretha Franklin at a concert in Connecticut, I was assigned the front stage position. The "God Spot" as it was called. No obstruction, no one in my way, just me and the Queen of Soul separated by only a few feet.

"If you're gonna get that close," she said to me, "don't you shoot up my nose."

"Not to worry," I said. "I'll shoot from the front row."

In my head the assignment was easy enough. Me and Aretha hanging out at the front of the stage. Me shooting. Her singing. Great shots. Great music. Great time for all.

In reality, not so great.

For starters, the front row seats were all taken. So I was forced to stand at the foot of the stage. I had assumed, incorrectly of course, that the stage would be no higher than a few inches. An intimate setting-in-the-round, so to speak. What I found was no "round" at all. Rather, a ballroom, which held nearly 1,000 people with a stage towering six feet high. The only place to shoot was from her feet. Directly up her nose. Directly in the spot I'd promised her I wouldn't be in.

Stage lights are blinding and it's often difficult to see the crowd in front of you. At least, this was the logic I used to convince my conscience that the position I had chosen was, in fact, a good one. "She'll never even see me," I thought.

If you don't know this by now, I'm seldom right.

Not only would I be angling my camera up her nostrils, I'd be using a wide-angle lens. It promised to be a less-than-flattering perspective.

As the band began playing, I moved into position. Slowly making my way toward the stage.

"R. E. S. P. E. C. T.," Aretha belted out. Looking directly into my lens, she continued. "Take that camera off of me!"

I knew her song pretty well. I couldn't, for the life of me, remember *that* line being in it.

Aretha lowered her mic, placed her hand on her hip, and quit singing entirely, never once breaking eye contact with me. I don't think she even blinked.

I looked around, feeling thousands of eyes fixated on me. It was like a late night interrogation in a dingy police station—two chairs and a table…a swinging lamp overhead…a pre-written confession being slid across the table in my direction while detectives watched in earnest from a one-way mirror.

If the band had been holding rocks, I think they would have seriously considered a public stoning. Before I allowed them an opportunity to find any, I lowered my camera and searched for the nearest escape.

The illuminated exit sign above a nearby doorway behind me seemed miles away. I moved toward it, and Aretha picked up at the next verse. It was all quite seamless, actually. The whole thing lasting no longer than three or four seconds, but for me, it felt like three years.

"Sock it to me. Sock it to me. Sock it to me. Sock it to me," I heard Aretha sing, as I made my way from the ballroom.

She certainly had. The crowd cheered madly. The band's horns blew furiously. And I began my search for a rock to crawl under.

Rocking the Boat with Natalie Cole

Causing one of the greatest singers of all time to stop a concert midstream is one of the most awkward things imaginable. Coming in at a close second is getting accused of harassment by another iconic vocalist and being thrown out of a star-studded party on a multi-million dollar yacht. Luckily for me, we were docked. Otherwise, my camera and I would have been tossed into the ocean with a tripod wrapped around my neck. Tony Soprano style.

The Atlantis on Paradise Island in Nassau, Bahamas, is a haven for the rich and famous. With high-stakes gambling and state-of-the-art accommodations, it's a resort of privilege, which meant vacationing there always provided the guest an opportunity for a celebrity sighting.

Capturing images of celebrities playing on property was a marketing bonanza The Atlantis relished. I'd worked celebrity parties there for years: Stevie Wonder's birthday, a weekend concert with the Jonas Brothers, a golf game between Bill Clinton and James Caan. Lindsay Lohan and

Paris Hilton dropped in whenever they were going through publicity withdrawals. It was always an easy assignment.

The VIP parties were not.

Those were celebrity respites designed for unwinding without cameras anywhere in sight. Of course, anytime The Atlantis marketing team realized a celebrity party was underway we would be dispatched to capture the backstage glamour.

The celebrities hated me being there but not nearly as much as I hated showing up. Since everything was paid for, they almost always allowed us access. It was an occupational hazard both sides endured.

One night I was assigned to cover a VIP party on a yacht. Natalie Cole had just finished a concert, and a job-well-done party was being thrown in her honor. I had these assignments down to a science. Get in quickly, find a low-profile location, hold the widest shot possible, and let the tape roll. Sooner or later, some famous person was bound to step in front of the lens. It usually took no more than five minutes. When that happened, I had my celebrity, and I could call it a night.

It was a fly-on-the-wall approach that had served me well over the years. However, I never stopped to think it may appear to someone unfamiliar with my approach (especially if I sat there for a lengthy period of time) that I was not, in fact, a cameraman for the resort trying to show a celebrity in a good light, but, rather, a stalker, intent on capturing celebrity dirt for the highest bidder.

Such was the case with Natalie Cole.

I made my way onto the yacht and squeezed into the corner of a nearby bulkhead. Famous actors and rock stars were everywhere. Ten feet away from where I'd perched, in the center of my line of sight, was Natalie. Propping myself against the wall, I hit record on my camera, stood, and waited for her to turn around. This was going to be easy. But something didn't seem quite right. She wasn't turning.

The boat was crowded and music and chatter filled every room. I couldn't hear a thing Natalie was saying. All I knew was that she was animated, her hands flying in every direction, engrossed in conversation.

"C'mon!" I said to myself. "Look at me. Smile. Anything. Just turn so I can go to bed."

For nearly twenty minutes, all I saw was Natalie's flailing arms and the back of her head. I took a step closer, hoping my movement might cause her to glance in my direction. And, like clockwork, she turned. We locked eyes. No smile. Just a familiar feeling I was, once again, in serious trouble. Then, two large hands came out of nowhere, wrapped themselves around my waist, and picked me up with surprising ease.

Now in the grip of a bodyguard, the absurdity of the scene was startling; my feet dangled a foot or so off the ground with a camera still resting on my shoulder. All of a sudden, everyone was looking at me, and the sea of star-studded faces parted as Brutus and I made our way to the exit.

Setting me down on the dock, his booming voice underscored the obvious. "You need to leave this boat! Now!"

"I think I am off," I said sarcastically. I realized—perhaps a tad too late—that I was shouting into his stomach. I craned my neck upward; he was bigger than a refrigerator. "I mean, okay. Sure. No problem."

I went to bed and decided not to mention any of this to my boss. After all, surely *someone* famous had walked past my camera. "It'll be fine," I told myself.

In the morning, we all met for breakfast.

"How was the party?" my boss asked me.

"Fine. No problems."

"Oh, really?" he countered. "Then do you mind explaining why you were harassing Natalie Cole, eavesdropping on her private conversation, arguing with a 300-pound bodyguard, and drinking from their bar?"

"Wait a second!" I said, defensively. "That is *so* not true. I *never* got a drink from the bar!"

Out of Sync with N'Sync

Most times, it's not the celebrity that presents difficulties. It's their handlers.

Once, on a commercial shoot at Walt Disney World, I was told by Christina Aguilera's handlers not to look her in the eyes. When she arrived on the set, she held out her hand and said, "Hello."

I didn't know what to do. Take it? Not take it? Walk way? I was confused, so I looked down and grunted something unintelligible. I think she thought I was a deaf mute.

Tony Bennett, who was most gracious, almost lost it when a baby cried during his set at the Ritz Carlton in Grand Cayman. But his handler played the bad guy for him.

"Who takes a baby to a Tony Bennett concert anyway?" he said to himself, under his breath. "Babies are meant to be *made* at a Tony Bennett show." With that, the handler escorted the family out of the venue.

But celebrities, despite being lavished with attention from handlers who never say "no" to them, are just like normal people. If, that is, you manage to catch them at just the right moment.

Once, in the middle of summer in Mexico, Sheryl Crow didn't bat an eye when I slipped a mic through her dress for an outside interview, only to reveal another "slip" entirely. "It's too hot to wear a bra," she said looking up at me. "Just clip the thing on. I don't care."

And Dolly Parton's famous assets were front and center during a live shot I did with her and Al Roker. With two crews covering the event, the audio operators flipped a coin to decide who'd be putting the mic on her. Paul won the toss.

Stepping toward Dolly, Paul's excitement turned to puzzlement as he struggled to figure out exactly where to place the thing. Surveying the entertainer's ultra-famous, double-platinum, larger than life icons, he inadvertently dropped the windscreen straight down her shirt. Afraid going in after it might result in a restraining order Paul, scratched his head in bewilderment. "Don't worry, honey," Dolly said with her trademark good-humor. "They won't bite."

It's usually one or the other, the celeb or the handler, that becomes the obstacle. But when *both* are upset with you, it's a fairly safe bet that you are, in fact, the impediment.

The Turks and Caicos are a spectacular chain of islands sandwiched between Miami and Puerto Rico. They have turquoise waters that lap against pristine, white, sandy beaches. And, in the fall of 2001, I got to see them for myself, traveling to the island with N'Sync, along with a group of fifty radio contest winners from around the country.

N'Sync's *PopOdyssey Tour* was coming to an end, and those fifty winners were taking advantage of an all-inclusive trip for a private concert on the island.

For four days, I ran around the beaches capturing everything that moved. Autograph sessions, beach events, and sandcastle contests. It was all outside, under the furnace of an unusually hot, tropical heat wave.

On the last day, the day of the concert, I'd had enough. I was spent. That day seemed longer than all the others combined. And we never stopped to eat. As the sun set, Johnny Wright, the band's manager, asked if we wanted to go to the after party. Royal, my producer, and I were famished. I don't think either of us even said yes! We just ran, straightaway, into the VIP tent on the beach.

Sprinting past security, I shouted, "I'm with the band!" as I proceeded to make my way inside.

I'd always wanted to say that.

We were the first ones in. In the center of the room sat a display of edible proportions, the likes of which I had never before seen. Crab claws as long as my legs and shrimp that were larger than my hand were spilling over the sides. Chips and dip were everywhere—a pot of gold at the end of a beautiful, rainbow. And I was on a seek-and-destroy mission.

Like a raccoon in a garbage can, I devoured as much food as possible, grabbing easy snacks before having my privileges revoked. Pieces of chips crumbled to the floor while a salty-tasting black dip leaked from both corners of my mouth. Royal had made his way over from the bar and was returning to snag a few chips.

"What the hell did you just do?" Royal asked with a flummoxed look on his face.

"What do you mean?" I replied, realizing the bowl in front of me was now empty. "Oh, sorry," I said. "Maybe there's more coming."

"It's not the chips!" Royal said. "It's the Beluga." He pointed to the corners of my mouth.

"Oh, you mean the dip?" I asked. "Big deal. Beluga dip. Who cares?"

"Uh, that would be Beluga *caviar*," said a voice from behind.

We both turned. It was Justin Timberlake.

Dip or caviar, either one, it was all gone. The last remnants were clinging to the corners of my mouth.

Apparently, I had managed to consume nearly $10,000 worth of the stuff, all by myself. Even more astonishing was the fact I'd done so in just under five minutes.

Facing Johnny Wright and the rest of the band, I recognized the look on all their faces. No one needed to say a word. It was the same stare I'd seen from Rod Stewart, Aretha Franklin, Natalie Cole, and even Tony Bennett.

"You know that look, right?" asked Royal.

I nodded. We left, returned to our rooms, and ordered room service.

CHAPTER 17

There's Something Fishy Going On In Dubai

"How do you think I got here? Fairy dust? I flew. Just like everyone else."

—Charlize Theron

I n the midst of the biggest economic crisis since the Great Depression, The Atlantis Resort in Dubai decided to throw a Grand Opening party. It wasn't something designed to flaunt in the face of a world going broke; the party just happened to coincide with the crisis.

The one billion dollar resort sits at the northern end of a manmade island shaped like a palm tree. The Atlantis, a "spectacle in the sand" mega-resort based on the Lost City, was a sight to behold. The "Bridge Suite"—the hotel's signature accommodation—connected the hotel's two buildings and cost $35,000 a night. "Ordinary" guestrooms begin at $800. With 130 acres of grounds, guests can trek through an underground aquarium, take a camel ride on the beach, enjoy a variety of water slides, or eat at a restaurant where fresh lobster swim in a tank behind you before being steamed and thrown on a plate in front of you.

The price tag for the private party was rumored to be nearly 20 million dollars. But the gleam seemed to be coming off the glam quickly, as the timing for such extravagance hardly seemed ideal.

The region known as the United Arab of Emirates was groaning under heavy debt and bank lending had been tightened, which delayed new developments and further impacted jobs. The world's markets were sinking to historic new lows. Still, here we were. Making money. And none of us were complaining about that. In fact, The Atlantis showed very little evidence of a global financial meltdown. Robert De Niro and Richard Branson strolled through the lobby daily and Dom Pérignon flowed everywhere. Glasses were never empty.

Outside, on an elaborate stage built above one of the many pools, Kylie Minogue performed a set of her pop classics, while the night sky blazed with the world's largest fireworks display—a spectacle visible as far away as the International Space Station.

I spent a week in Dubai documenting the party and capturing the grand opening. The evening of the finale, I was assigned the "house camera" on the Red Carpet—"first position." A hundred or so cameras lined up to my left with each celebrity being instructed to stop at my location first.

We asked the usual questions: "How do you like the resort?" and "What's your favorite part?"

As a final question, we were told to ask how each celebrity got here because both Virgin Atlantic and Emirates had paid big bucks to shuttle the VIPs back and forth.

Everyone who walked the red carpet was asked this question. Everyone.

And they all answered in kind: "I flew on Virgin Atlantic!" or "I flew on Emirates!" Both declarations were followed by something like, "And the accommodations were *just wonderful!*"

Occasionally, one of the celebrities would ask me, "Didn't *you* think so?"

"Of *course!*" I said, pretending I had traveled in such luxury. Truth be told, I wanted to state what was *really* on my mind. Something like: "Listen, you got a $10,000 first class seat with a portable HD TV flat screen that magically popped out of your arm rest at the push of a button. Of *course* it was '*just wonderful!*' Who cares if the remote control didn't work because you were seated too far from the screen? You had free alcohol. And your seat splayed out into a queen size bed. It must have been '*just wonderful*' wrapping the 2,000 thread count Egyptian sheets around your body while you got your feet rubbed and cucumber slices laid over your eyelids."

Not that I'm bitter or anything …

"Still, while I'm ranting, let me tell you how *just wonderful* my experience was. How I wedged my way into a modern-day coach seat, shoehorning myself out, and back in, each time I had to go to the bathroom. How I spent the better part of six hours banging on the seat rest in front of me because my four-inch TV screen was broken. How I had to take a second mortgage on my home just to pay for the alcohol I bought during the fourteen-hour flight. And did I mention my seat was the last one in back?"

My ranting went on only in my head; my celebrity counterparts would never know any of my sad aeronautical tale. While they glowed and gloated, I smiled back and played the part.

Most of the celebrities came from Bollywood. I knew none of them. But I knew what Richard Branson looked like and Janet Jackson's bright smile was certainly familiar.

There wasn't a celebrity who didn't stop by my camera position. Each one was more than happy to talk with me.

Then ... there was Charlize Theron, who floated in on a cloud of glamour and grace.

"Is this where I'm supposed to stop?" she asked one of her handlers. Beauty aside, she didn't sound very happy about stopping there ... or anywhere for that matter.

The handler leaned into her ear. "Yeah. It'll be quick. Don't worry."

Raya, my producer, began with the proverbial, "What's your favorite part, so far?" question.

"I don't have one yet," Charlize said, firing back before the dot was even placed at the bottom of Raya's question mark. "I just got here."

"Ooooh ... kaaaay," replied Raya. Recognizing we may have gotten off to a bit of a shaky start, but ever confident we could still pull it out, Raya continued, "How'd you get here, then?"

Looking at us as if Raya just asked for the number to 911, she said, "How do you *think* I got here? Fairy dust? I flew. Just like everyone else."

She rolled her eyes as she turned to leave. She didn't bother to stop at any of the other cameras positions.

"What the hell was that?" Raya asked me.

"Nothing useable," I said. "Maybe she got stuck in economy like the rest of us."

Theron was the last interview of the night; Raya and I were both bummed we'd ended on a low point.

The following morning at brunch, our executive producer Duncan, explained why Charlize was in such a bad mood.

"*Was* she stuck in coach?" I asked.

"Uh, no. Not quite," he said.

He went on to explain that Charlize had taken a late flight and was pretty tired. She was given an underground aquarium room, an expensive luxury suite where one could draw back the curtains and gaze at the 65,000 different species of animal life that lived behind the glass.

While settling in, Charlize noticed a scuba diver feeding the fish. Triggerfish are fairly aggressive and tend to dart about rather quickly. While feeding the larger fish, the triggerfish kept getting in the way, trying to eat the food. To keep them at bay, the diver used one of his fins, placing a small school of triggerfish between his rubber flipper and a rock. Charlize, a huge PETA supporter, saw it and began banging on the glass for the diver to lift his flipper.

The glass in those rooms is curved and several inches thick, making it difficult to pull focus on anything. To the diver, it just looked like another guest, waving at him from their overpriced room. Trained to wave back, he did. While doing so, his flipper inadvertently began squishing the fish. Seeing this only enraged Charlize further. Pounding louder, with both fists, she pointed to the fish guts that were now floating throughout the tank. The diver, apparently unaware of the pieces of triggerfish floating past him, waved back. This time using both arms.

It was an image she couldn't shake.

None of us knew if the story was true. But after Duncan finished telling it, the waiter appeared and ran through the menu items. We listened intently, salivating as he rattled off a list of Mediterranean delights. When he got to the fish specials, Duncan and I both started to lose it.

By the time he had reached the end, we were laughing too hard to even order.

CHAPTER 18

Floating from Finland to Florida

Guest: "Excuse me, I have a question."

Cruise Official: "Yes, sir?"

Guest: "Where does the water in the pools come from?"

Cruise Official: "We actually convert seawater into freshwater and put it into the pools."

Guest: "Oh, so that's why the water's splashing so much!"

—A real conversation from a real person
to a real cruise line employee. *Really...*

I n the winter of 2009, I was asked to document, day-to-day, the crossing of one of the world's largest cruise ships. I'd been working on the buildup to the launch for nearly a year, and this—the voyage to its new port—was the final cherry on top of an enormous ice cream sundae.

I started the voyage in Finland and sailed 6,000 miles in just over a month. Remarkably, I was able to keep track of all the funny, ridiculous, and incredible moments along the way.

There Be a Ship!

It was a two-hour bus ride from Helsinki to Turku, where our ship sat in port. The locals told us the route was quite scenic, but we had to take their word for that. Rolling fog and light drizzle blocked our view of any landscapes.

Over his shoulder, our driver shouted at us in a jumbled stream of grunts and vowels, leaving me to wish I knew what he meant. Were his words those of reassurance or warning? I couldn't tell. All I knew was, the exclamations appeared to be urgent and he had gone from one side of the road to the other, both which left me nervous. Perhaps seeing the fear in my eyes, he quickly refocused his attention to the road and sharply swerved back into the proper lane.

Outside held ten-foot visibility and a temperature of twenty-eight degrees. Which, according to my calculations, made it legally freezing. The rain picked up, throwing itself at us sideways, hitting the tiny windows with such force, I thought the glass might shatter at any moment. Gusts of wind tugged at the trees, bending them like giant rubber pencils. We were a double-decker roller coaster on 18-wheels, teetering from side to side. I found myself ridiculously thankful I was far too tired to succumb to nausea.

Our ride had room for just over a hundred people, but there were only four of us on the bus. Each of us too jet-lagged to speak. So we spread out across the two-by-two seats. Legs stretched outward toward the roof, flat against the cold, wet bus windows. I closed my eyes, dreaming of sunshine and warm weather, as our bus swayed along.

Then my legs fell asleep.

As the bus pulled into the port, the four of us sat up and started gathering our gear, all the while staring out the window where our new seafaring ride was tethered to the dock with thick ropes and massive cables. Large cranes hovered over it. She was a real beauty. Eighteen stories high. Spit-shined and gleaming, even in the rain and bitter cold.

Pointing toward the open bus doors, our driver shouted a mixture of Cave Man and Klingon.

"Okh nejeck hook kcha!"

For such a pretty and intelligent people, the Finnish have a language that creates such contradictions between my eyes and ears.

I made my way to the front of the bus but refused to get out until I had a little more information. "Where do we go?" I futilely asked. "Do you know who we're supposed to meet?"

Further spewing unintelligible jargon, he rattled on and on. I couldn't understand a word. I'd managed better in Israel with the language of throat clearing and dramatic hand gestures.

Sensing my confusion, the driver scribbled something on a piece of paper and handed it to me.

Hieroglyphics would have been better.

I looked up at my traveling companions, who were shuffling nervously behind me. "I don't understand a word of this," I said.

The driver waved a finger in the direction of the ship; we took that as a universal sign to mean the hospitality was over. It was time for us to get out. Apparently, getting us *to* the ship was his job but getting us *on board* was not.

We grabbed our belongings, stacked the cases of equipment onto a pushcart, and made our way across the dock. The rain had lightened but continued to fall. We wandered around aimlessly, wet and with no idea of how to get *onto* the ship. Workers ran around us with tools, hard hats, and determined attitudes with facial expressions that told us we were something close to trespassers. Or worse: the entertainment.

Climbing through an open door at the back of the ship, we finally managed our way aboard and were given the keys to our staterooms. When I put my key into the door, I was surprised to see my attendant sitting on the couch, watching TV. He greeted me in Finnish with such conviction and intensity, I couldn't tell if he was inviting me for tea or denouncing me as a fascist. *Nothing* made sense.

"You wouldn't happen to speak Hebrew would you?" I asked.

To which he stared.

My dilemma had only just begun.

Having traveled to dozens of countries over the years, languages and dialects have always been easy for me to grow accustomed to, but not at the same time. I'd never heard so many languages spoken in one place, at once, in all my life. There was Italian, French, Spanish, Bulgarian, Chinese, German, Arabic, Dutch, and Portuguese. It was a floating United Nations. And I was getting ready to sail without a translator.

Welcome Aboard!

The most amazing thing about Superman was not that he could bend steel or stop bullets, but that he could change so quickly in a phone booth. My shower was about the same size and I could barely bathe, much less change my clothes and leap tall buildings in a single bound. It didn't take me long to realize the bumps and thuds I heard while walking down the corridors in the morning were not the sounds of the ship workers but, rather, elbows and heads banging their way into the hard plastic capsule-like shower walls.

When we arrived—and for the first week we were on board—our ship was still a work in progress. There was a never-ending parade of workers moving on and off the ship at all hours. We went about our daily grind alongside them. An incessant noise of drilling and pounding and the smell of fresh paint wafting through each and every corridor became an expected part of the experience.

Accommodation-wise (other than the showers), we had it made: four staterooms next to each other with one large suite for our editing equipment, cases, cameras, and lights. While we shot the stories each day, our editor remained in his "bat cave," a suite of approximately 1000 square feet. This lap of luxury featured two bathtubs, a wrap around balcony, three bedrooms, and a living room large enough to dance the polka.

Unfortunately, said glorious suite didn't have electricity, which meant no heat or hot water. Each day, our editor worked away while dressed in multiple layers of clothing and a ski cap. We connected his power under the door of an adjoining room. Once, when he blew a power strip after connecting it to a bad socket, we all gathered around the smoking instrument for what little warmth it afforded.

Each of us had our own issues to deal with. For whatever reason, the workers had no problem walking into any room they felt like going into, and without knocking. Not much of a problem if the room is empty. But let's say—merely for the sake of entertainment—that a guest is standing naked, brushing his teeth, all while singing an ABBA song. And then let's say, again for same said argument, that "the guest" strolled out of his bathroom, only to look up and find an attendant whose name he can't pronounce, fluffing the pillows on his bed.

Well, if that were true—and I'm not saying it is—it was certainly an interesting way to start the day.

An Icy and Exhilarating Kiss Goodbye

About a week into our assignment, just before four in the morning, we awoke to begin our voyage. Our ship would soon pull away from its berth, ready to take up new residence in the warmer climate of South Florida.

We made our way topside around half past five to capture the ship pulling away from the dock. The process, although a technological marvel, does not happen quickly. Pulling a ship that size away from a dock takes time and patience. Capturing the moment on video isn't easy either. I found myself sliding across the icy deck in the darkened cold while my teeth chattered around my chapped lips like miniature jackhammers.

I tend to lose interest within seconds when action is lacking. But capturing the excitement of a "four-years-in-the-making" moment while watching mist slowly roll off the tops of the ice-cold Finnish water and blinking at the sun as it creeps above the treetops is utterly exhilarating.

Until that moment, I believed humans had no business living this far north. Only sea lions, fish, and fluffy white polar bears should inhabit a place this frigid. But as I watched for "first light" to arrive, the stars radiating in the clear, morning sky and the lights of the ship bouncing off the glassy water, I witnessed the true beauty of the upper part of the globe and finally began to understand its allure.

After a little over an hour, we had our story. Shaking off the cold while entering the warmth of the captain's bridge, the fact we were experiencing this rare opportunity at all was not lost on any of us. After witnessing something so incredible, the midnight intrusions, cold showers, and freezing weather suddenly became a price worth paying. We began to appreciate everything, taking nothing for granted.

Then our TV cut out, the Internet went down again, snowflakes fell, and we cursed the world from Finland to Florida and back again.

With two weeks from home and heading toward some spectacular places, I located a map on the bridge and plotted our course with a few of the officers standing nearby. We were floating in the Baltic Sea, just off the coast of Sweden, a little north of Stockholm. I was aboard one of the largest cruise ships in the world and Estonia and Latvia were just to my east. Poland was due south, about a day away. We'd be sailing around the tip of Copenhagen, heading north toward Norway, into the North Sea, and skirting the coast of England for about a day. Then we'd eventually make our way through the English Channel, sailing just to the north of France and heading straight into the Atlantic for home.

I pinched myself just to make sure I was really there.

Clearing a Crucial Obstacle:

Cruising into Korsoer, Denmark, we had one way to go: through a narrow strait. It required passing under the Danish Great Belt Fixed Link Bridge, which runs between the Danish islands of Zealand and Funen. For most ships, passing under bridges isn't usually a big deal. But there were, in fact, some "issues" presented to us with this particular structure.

Our ship stood just over 70 meters. The Great Belt Bridge—massive as it is—stands at *only* 65 meters. I didn't need a calculus professor to see the problem. Knowing full well we'd be stuck in the Baltic Sea unless we made it under the bridge, the engineers designed an ingenious way to clear the crucial obstacle: retractable smokestacks.

I was told that the lowering of the funnels is a four-hour process, but more than necessary, as the Captain told us, "to squeeze under the bridge and head into the North Sea." It turns out "squeezing" wasn't an exaggeration.

Just after midnight, we caught sight of the bridge. Cruising at just over 20 knots, the most ominous part of the approach (other than the fact we might crash into a pillar) was that the center of the Great Belt, the part we were heading toward, was cast into complete darkness. Only the east and west bridge supports were visible.

Around 1:30, we were within two hundred yards of the bridge. With Danish officials showing tremendous confidence by halting traffic on the Great Belt and hundreds of people watching from the cold and darkened nearby beaches (don't these people sleep?), we began our glide underneath.

The strategy included gaining speed to press us deeper into the water. It was a technique designed to gain more clearance, but it also increased the peril.

It happened quickly, with the massive concrete structure zooming overhead within the slimmest of margins. From the top of the deck, the underneath of the bridge seemed close enough to touch, and if you were standing atop the retracted smokestacks, you very well could have. There was a half-meter gap between us and the bottom of the Great Belt.

This maneuver had been the talk of the ship for days and I'd paid very little attention. But, after watching these folks take a behemoth vessel like ours—225,000 tons and nearly 1,200 feet long—and figure out a way to cram it under a bridge with only two-foot of clearance while I have trouble pulling my car into the garage is nothing short of spectacular.

Once past the bridge, we headed north, sailing through the North Sea in the direction of Norway. We'd made a horseshoe turn south toward the Netherlands then glided our way straight towards the English Channel.

"The Channel is always unpredictable," the Captain told us. "Things could get pretty choppy."

A storm had recently moved in, which meant possible twenty-foot waves greeting us upon our arrival. However, we were still several days away and we'd had nothing but smooth sailing thus far. So we put it out of our minds and concerned ourselves with practicing our Finnish.

The Channel: From Windless To Windy

We'd known only calm, glassy waters on this trip, so it was quite a shock to see gale force winds picking up just before nightfall. With gusts of nearly 70 miles per hour, we were officially experiencing tropical-force conditions. The captain had been wrong about the twenty-foot waves. They were nearly twice that size and crashing against the Deck 4 dining room windows. Throngs of people excitedly strained to catch a glimpse of the water sloshing against the portholes. Half an hour later, like drunkards looking for a place to lie down, their excitement turned to angst as they stumbled down hallways and smashed into walls in search of either a bed or a bathroom. It was like Stevie Wonder leading a conga line.

This was our welcome to the English Channel.

I woke the next morning with my head buried in my pillow and flat on the floor of my stateroom. Having been pitched off the bed several times, I'd decided to remain there. I had fallen asleep to the sounds of an angry storm buffeting the ship. But, when I woke, only silence surrounded me. I stepped onto my balcony and looked out. Staring into blue skies and full sun, I noticed a long line of chalky cliffs lining the landscape to my right. Time stood still for me as I gazed into The White Cliffs of Dover.

I grabbed my iPod and played Jimmy Cliff's, *Many Rivers to Cross*. Once again, dumbfounded that I was there. On this ship. Looking at the cliffs. On this balcony. The boy from Fenton who hadn't known Jethro Tull from Jethro Clampett.

The picturesque postcard day didn't last nearly long enough. As we sat just off the English coast, the sun was setting, and the rain picked up again. We were making our way into the Northern Atlantic.

Checking the charts, I noticed we were near the Azores, about 900 miles off the coast of Lisbon. We were sailing past the English and French hillsides, and I was fully aware that would be the last stretch of land we'd see for at least ten more days. I worked hard to memorize them.

As The Stomach Turns

Making our way out of the Channel and into the rough and icy North Atlantic waters, I was reminded of years before when I'd flown on NASA's "Vomit Comet" airplane. Appropriately nicknamed, it was a specially modified Boeing 707 that performed a series of parabolic maneuvers. The KC 135, as it was officially designated, was designed to train astronauts in weightless conditions. Ron Howard used the very same plane for his zero gravity scenes in the movie *Apollo 13*. I'd even heard Tom Hanks talk about vomiting in it.

Much like the bend at the end of a wire coat hanger, the plane climbs at a steep angle of attack, pulling 2G's as it ascends. As the plane pushes over for its steep 45-degree decent, the arc it creates allows for all the contents in the plane to fall at the same rate of speed, giving roughly thirty seconds of weightlessness before the pilot pulls out of the dive and back to straight and level flight. Then, the process is repeated. Several times over. It's a wondrous ride at five miles in the air.

Over the years, I'd flown hundreds of parabolas, the first, by far, the most memorable. Along with veteran astronaut Pete Conrad, two astronauts-in-training, and a group of other journalists, I boarded the plane for the ultimate experience. For nearly two hours, the plane did exactly what it was supposed to do: climb up and push over, up and over, up and over. With each parabola, we floated, flipped, and bounced off the walls. Pete Conrad proved "once an astronaut, always an astronaut." The "newbies" proved they could work in a zero-g environment. And I proved that weightlessness and a full stomach do not go hand-in-hand.

My stateroom on the ship sat about a hundred feet above sea level. As I woke to greet the North Atlantic, I got the same feeling of nausea I'd experienced with Pete Conrad at 36,000 feet.

We were 70 miles off the coast of France, but I couldn't see it. Two consecutive days of sixty-knot howling winds, and fifty-foot waves had been crashing into us relentlessly. Like the creaking sounds of an old house, there was a constant noise emanating from every corner of the vessel, reminding me of the frailty of even the world's *largest* cruise ships. There was a consistent whistle from the sliding glass doorways. Water splashed about in the toilets and closet doors were opening and closing like angry poltergeists. Earlier in the day, a ceiling tile fell off in our edit bay, crashing into our monitor and knocking it to the floor. At lunch, I caught a bottle of vinegar as it slid across the table in my direction. The scene reminded me of Clint Eastwood or John Wayne, catching the whiskey shot glass sliding from the other side of the bar at the saloon.

There was no way I could look through a viewfinder, for fear of reprising my role from NASA's "vomit comet." We decided to take a break. Although, there was little I could do to escape the unremitting rocking—sitting, standing, falling into the bed, or burying my head into another pillow. Nothing worked.

"Drink Sprite," the captain told me. "It works for pregnant women; surely it can work for you."

I decided I'd just as well *be* pregnant than go through much more of this. Just as I was about to grab one from the counter, I remembered Pete Conrad's advice: "Make sure you eat a full breakfast," he said before we boarded NASA's puke mobile.

I left the Sprite unopened.

Coming to America

After days of zigging and zagging our way through storms across the Northern Atlantic, we finally turned south toward the Florida coastline. I was going home!

The storm had forced us to continue tracking west; at one point we were about 200 miles off the coast of Ireland, a place we weren't supposed to be anywhere near.

Our ship was loaded with all the latest and greatest in oceanic technology. One such piece of equipment, the Wave Meter, sat along the bow, measuring the height of all the waves and swells. The data is transmitted to the bridge, where its readings are posted in seconds. At some point during the storm, the pounding rendered the Wave Meter useless. Workers had to reassemble it so as to decipher its results. The data told us the winds we experienced during the storm were, in fact, hurricane strength. The Wave Meter measuring waves as high as 80 feet.

From the bridge looking down, it was difficult to gauge their height by using just our eyes. However, the bow is seven decks up, and we saw plenty of waves crashing over her.

Following the Family Footprint

It had been nine days since we left the English Channel and the last bit of land we'd seen. We passed the Azores, but it was at night and I was busy staring at the inside of my eyelids. Next up was Bermuda, an island we also sailed by in total darkness.

A funny thought came then. Remembering the Channel and the northern coast of France, I was reminded of my family's Atlantic crossing at the beginning of World War I. I remembered hearing stories of how they crammed themselves into steerage class accommodations aboard the *RMS Carmania*, an armed merchant cruiser less than 700 feet long. My grandmother told stories of how the family chugged across the English Channel on their way to a new land. A future.

I was sailing through those same waters and feeling a bit nostalgic. Staring out into the vast, open waters ahead, I recalled passing Le Harve, France, the port my family boarded from. I imagined all the similarities of our journeys, how we each took a ship across the Atlantic.

And that's where the likenesses ended.

Having faith wasn't my problem. Recognizing it existed and knowing how to tap into it was. But that had not been an issue for my family.

Earlier that summer, Sue and I took our daughter Lauren to New York and spent an entire afternoon at the archives on Ellis Island. Combing through pages of documents we learned all about my family's journey. According to the ship's manifest, they came with $13.52. I had a Sea Pass Card that didn't swipe correctly when I ordered my glass of wine. They took whatever discomfort came their way without complaint. I made sure everyone within 1200 feet knew of my unpleasantness.

Every member of my family was squeezed together in third class without amenities. Whereas my bed went unmade for two days (you should have heard me gripe about that!), twice my duvet was crooked (again, this was not acceptable), three times the audio on the TV was stuck, twice I had to phone the concierge because my air conditioner wouldn't turn off, and once my hairdryer broke.

My family never changed clothes. I complained to my personal stateroom attendant because my laundry took three days to get cleaned.

My family traveled in the winter with no heat. Okay. So *here* we actually came close to having near-identical experiences.

They wrote letters and waited to get to Ellis Island for postal delivery. I communicated with my friends and family via the Internet. I Skyped. I listened to music on my iPod. If I needed to know more about my location, I "Googled" it.

They ate rice, noodles, and bread. I dined on Chateaubriand.

After sailing nearly 6,000 miles of ocean, I knew that when I set foot on dry land I'd have all the conveniences my family never dreamed possible. There would be a car waiting to take me to the airport, a Skycap greeting me at curbside ready to take my bags, and an airplane would fly me home. I'd meet someone at baggage claim and fall into a warm bed at day's end. There'd be food in my refrigerator, wine in the credenza, and the lawn and pool services will have come and gone multiple times. And, after a few weeks, I'd get a check in the mail for the work I did on the crossing.

And what struck me most of all was this: not *one* of those things would have been possible had my family's difficult journey in 1914 not been made. They had courage and determination. But above all else, they had faith. Without it, they would have never boarded that ship. And I would have never existed.

Eventually, I knew I'd grumble again, when a red light takes too long to change or the checkout line in the market is ten deep. But, on that ship, after thinking of what my family did almost 100 years before, I decided not to be angry if the airport shuttle was late, or if the Skycap wasn't quick enough, or if the flight home took too long to load its passengers. If the refrigerator was void of food or if my bottles of wine were in need of restocking, that'd be fine. If the lawn care and pool service missed a week, well, that was okay too.

For the moment, at least, hurricane force winds and 80-foot waves were insignificant impediments when compared to the sacrifices my family endured. I may have sailed in their path, but they were the ones who set the course for my future.

And that, truly, is how I got here.

With or without the M&Ms.

———

Faith is older than humanity. It's more than a series of rites and rituals. I began to understand that while living in the Middle East—an adventure that had shaken and stirred me more than a Bond martini. There, I had broken down the denominational boundaries and questioned the puzzling opposition between religion and spirituality.

I now recognize that my family of immigrants was part of an ancestral DNA that helped create my unique inner conflict. But where does this faith thing take me? What do I do with it now?

I don't know. I still don't have the answers. Not all of them, anyway. But I do know that faith is the F-word that will carry me through my ongoing peace process.

Epilogue

"Congratulations! Today is your day.
You're off to great places! You're off and away!"

—Dr. Seuss

And with those words, my daughter Lauren graduated high school and went to college. Her mom and I moved her into her 5th floor dormitory, a room, which quickly became a fully functioning mini command center. Cable TV, a coffeemaker, high-speed internet access, and a laptop with a built-in camera no bigger than the tip of a ballpoint pen. We left, confident in her ability to run a small war without ever having to get up from her chair.

When I was in college, my letters were handwritten. I licked stamps and used White Out when I made mistakes. Half a week was normal for the post to travel from Charleston to St. Louis. Once, when my response to the latest argument my mom and I were having arrived in her hands, so much time had passed, we'd both completely forgotten we were fighting.

Lauren's generation may have many technological marvels at their fingertips but, as far as I'm concerned, growing up in the Midwest in the '80's was much easier than the fast-paced world of today. We were challenged to be creative and we had a lot of fun!

We played outside and, when forced to remain indoors, we dreamed. Each of us pictured ourselves in the rich stories told by our teachers, who wrote on chalkboards and showed films on projectors. Our imaginations took us to exotic, faraway places like Jefferson City, Missouri, and Springfield, Illinois.

We saw pictures in magazines of computers the size of refrigerators that only governments possessed. Music came on vinyl. Personalized cell phones, multi-line call waiting, and voicemail didn't exist. If you called someone while they were talking to someone else, you got a busy signal. If they were gone, the phone just rang and rang. No answering machine. No voicemail.

Life was much less complicated. We adored its simplicity.

We stayed out until dark, doors were never locked, and we drank water from hoses with our lips resting on the metallic nozzle. We played baseball in the streets. Mailboxes became first and third base with a Frisbee or trashcan lid for second.

We swore oaths to secret tree-fort clubs girls weren't allowed to know about. Then, we hit puberty, and Lisa Teeburg became our club president.

Every kid traded baseball cards after devouring the roofing-like material the trading card companies called bubble gum. Our toys were simple. My Slinky, for instance; a silver, helical spring of wire that was supposed to walk down entire flights of stairs, hardly ever made more than two at a time before crashing or stopping altogether. It was magical and monotonous, often at the same time.

I was shaped by the simplicity of the era in which I grew up. The imaginative fuel of my youth helped launch twenty years of adventure. It was fertile ground for a career that provided a collection of indelible experiences. Drinking coffee with Tony Bennett. Dancing with Oprah Winfrey. Eating tortilla chips with Robin Williams and Lisa Marie Presley while watching whales breech in the Sea of Cortez. Spending time in a bathroom with Walter Cronkite. And, a few years later, finding myself doing the same thing with Tom Cruise, humming Bob Seager's *Old Time Rock and Roll* at the urinal next to his. I believe Mr. Cruise left mid-stream. Truly one of my weaker moments.

Often times I found myself at the center of historical events, face-to-face with presidents and prime ministers, with front-row seats on world stages across five continents.

I'll get to those other two eventually.

It's unnecessary to be imaginative today. Live-streaming video, available in the palm of our hands, allows the world to come to us. Why bother to travel to France or to the top of the planet's highest summit when views from the Eiffel Tower and Mt. Everest are readily available in 360-degree high-def splendor?

While it's easy to see the world from a laptop, it's not nearly as enriching. Technology has allowed us an opportunity to *see* experiences—*viewing*, not *doing*. It's virtual versus authentic, the difference between visiting Italy online and drinking coffee in St. Mark's Square in Venice.

Marvelous moments happen to us all the time. We're just usually not present enough to be aware of them while their happening. Experiences feed a curiosity that carries you beyond your backyard, to find wonders big and small. Near and far. Extraordinary and ordinary. You can find adventure everywhere and anytime. Even late in your own game.

"And will you succeed?
Yes! You will indeed!
(98 and ¾ percent guaranteed.)"

Lastly, a quick thanks:

Thank you, Eva Marie Everson, for all your editing and words of wisdom—and to Jonathan Clements, my agent. Thank you, both of you, for your friendship, your tireless work, and yes … faith! Thank you, for enduring my ridiculous questions, never ending phone calls and rambling text messages. And to all those who have come in and out of my life all these many years—you know who you are. I send a nearly half century's worth of thanks! You've supplied me with an endless stream of unforgettable memories.

Lastly, Lastly—About the Author:

Dan Beckmann worked as a cameraman for NBC News for 15 years. While on staff in Tel Aviv, he helped cover the continuation of the Middle East Peace Process. His travels have taken him throughout Europe, Asia, and the Middle East, helping NBC cover a wide range of stories: from the Olympics in Torino, to coverage of 9-11 at Ground Zero, Hurricane Katrina, and presidential campaigns aboard Air Force One. Aside from The Today Show, Dateline, Nightly News with Brian Williams, and MSNBC, Dan's work has also been featured on Good Morning America, ESPN, CBS News, CNN, National Geographic, A&E, the BBC, and many other programs worldwide.

Dan is an accomplished columnist, speaks four languages, flies airplanes, loves wine and plays the piano badly. Most likely a result of the wine.

He's traveled a long way from Fenton, Missouri.

CPSIA information can be obtained at www.ICGtesting.com
Printed in the USA
BVOW03s2157010514

352122BV00002B/4/P

9 781630 470562